5 Weeks Learning to Draw

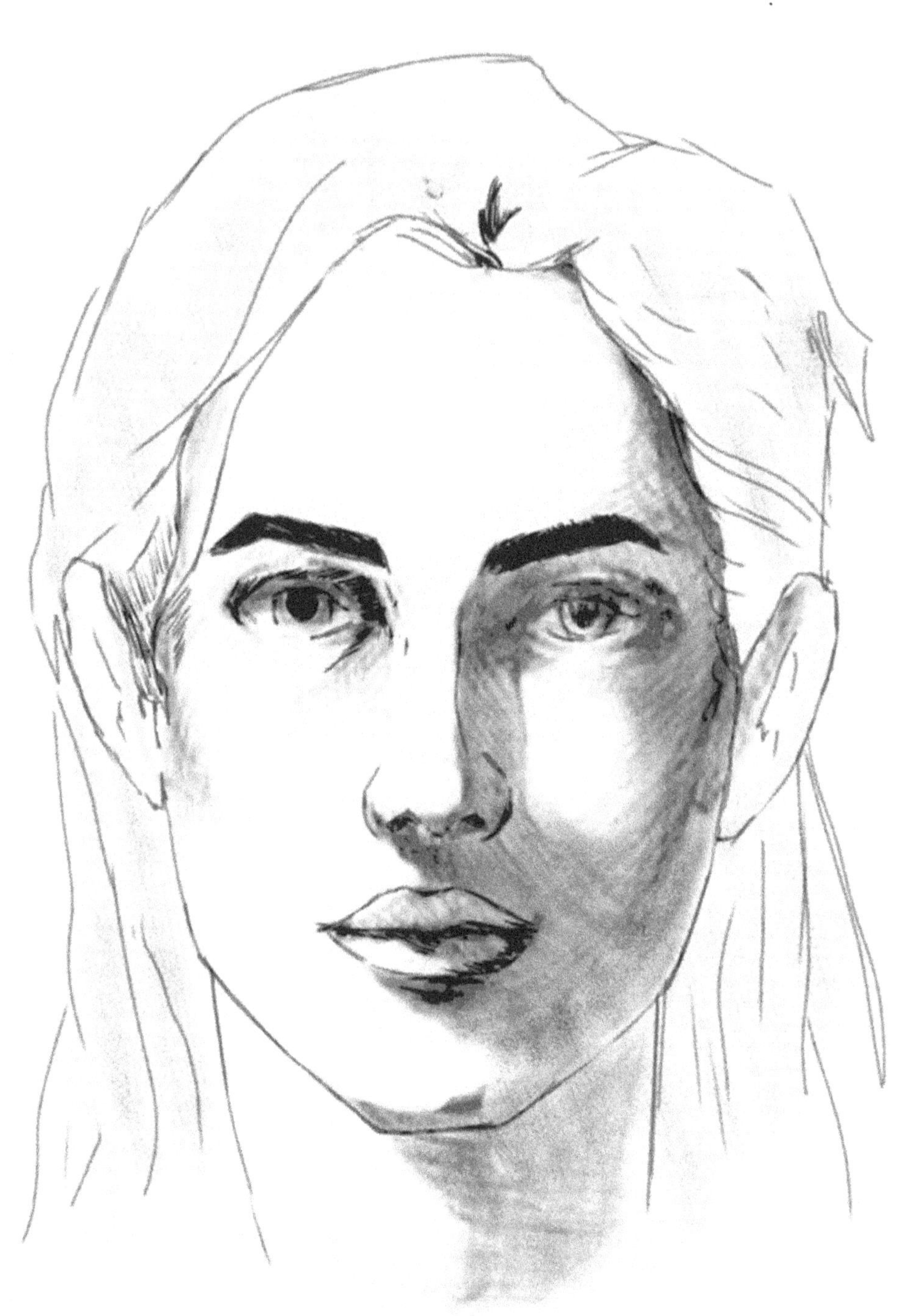

5 Weeks Learning to Draw

Drawing with Step By Step Instructions on How to Draw Different Everyday Objects

(Animals, Plants, Humans)

Martha Folsbee

Group Product Manager: Abisayo Emmanuel
Senior Editor: Tanya D'cruz
Technical Editor: Arjun Varma
Project Coordinator: Segun Saini
Proofreader: Ayo Editing
Illustrator: Jallow
Published by Cactus Publishing House LLC.
30 N Gould St Ste R
Sheridan
82801, Wyoming

DEDICATION

To Alan

Love you now and always!

(How does it feel to be in a book!!)

To my amazing sons, George and Tobi: There genuinely are no words. I'm proud of you all and I love you all very much.

TABLE OF CONTENTS

PREFACE

Hello and Congratulations!

If you've picked up this book, you're intrigued by the prospect of learning to draw and being known as an artist. This book can be viewed as a five-week diary in which, if divided into twenty to thirty minutes of learning per day, you can learn to draw beautiful pictures easily.

Anyone, regardless of skill level, can start learning to draw. Even if you have no artistic background, practice and a willingness to learn will help you improve your sketching skills and discover your creative potential.

This book is all about breaking things down into fundamental forms and then sketching those using pencils. It offers simple step-by-step pictures that are simple to follow. Don't get discouraged by early setbacks or compare yourself to others. Everyone's artistic journey is unique, and the joy of drawing comes from expressing your own unique perspective and style. Enjoy the process and allow yourself to make mistakes—mistakes are crucial for growth and learning.

Are you prepared to embark on this incredible journey?

Let the creative voyage begin!

COMMON MISCONCEPTIONS ABOUT DRAWING

1. Its Difficult

The idea that sketching is difficult is the most common misconception I encounter. You're either born with the ability to draw like Picasso or you're left struggling.

The reality is much more different because talent originates from interest and consistency. As you practice and become more familiar with an activity, it gets easier. You need only do the following need to schedule practice time.

2. I do not have enough time

The excuse that one is too busy to learn how to draw is another widespread fallacy. It may feel like there's no way you can fit anything else into your busy schedule and other commitments.

The book's exercises are tailored intended to take no longer than a few minutes each day. Try to find a fixed time every day to go through this book at a certain location that you call your workspace. Once you commit to thirty minutes, you may find yourself inspired to spend even more time practicing!

3. it's too expensive

The tasks in this book are intended to be performed with simple drawing supplies, easy to locate and reasonably priced. Basic tools such as a pencil, paper, and eraser some of these things you probably have in your own home right now.

4. it's not productive

Taking up a new interest as an adult is sometimes met with feelings of guilt. It's a common misconception that drawing is pointless and a waste of time. This is not true, studies find that drawing helps you in unexpected ways. You can let your imagination run wild while you draw.

You may temporarily ignore all of life's stresses and worries while you concentrate on the fundamentals of drawing, such as line, shape, form, value, space, and texture. You'll become a more perceptive observer as you hone your drawing abilities.

With all these great benefits, there’s nothing left to hold you back.

HOW TO USE THIS BOOK

There are steps-by-step illustrations, techniques, photos, and instructions. Every illustration in this book is intended to be drawn again. I advise using our 5 Week Learn to draw drawing notebook for this.

Although there will be blank practice sheets available, I'm assuming you'd like to practice again on various pages until you're happy with the outcome. So, we have created a blank sketchpad journal to help you keep up with your practice drawings. Simply search on Amazon for 'Everyone can draw in 5 Weeks' journal.

MATERIALS YOU'LL NEED

These materials are easily accessible online or in the art department of your local craft store.

1. **Drawing paper**; an absolute necessity for all painters. It is recommended to use a simple blank journal with at least fifty blank pages rather than a simple bundle of printed paper.

2. **A daily planner or alarm clock**: You'll only need to set aside 20 minutes every day to sketch with me. I'd recommend picking a time that you can commit to for the entire 5 weeks and has uninterrupted time. Your mind would then become accustomed to this habit and "remind" you to paint at a specific time each day. You can set a basic alarm on your phone for 5 weeks.

3. **Pencils:** For rough sketches that are easier to edit, use a wood HB pencil. Although shading and producing value with colored pencils can be difficult, pushing the pen tip firmly or softly will create better results.

4. **Cleaners:** The best erasers to use are the Pentel Hi-Polymer eraser for rough erasing and the Prisma color Kneaded Rubber eraser for selective erasing. Choose the option that most appeals to you. Examine a few to see what kinds of traces they leave. Lead may spread more when it softens, which you may not like.

5. **Sharpeners**: I prefer a disposable sharpener that is portable.

6. **Rulers**: Purchase a clear plastic ruler so you can see the artwork while drawing lines.

7. **Your Working Environment**: When you first start drawing, you want an area that is free of distractions, has a comfortable chair, and lots of light. You want to be able to notice what is going on and focus on the task at hand right away.

TEST YOURSELF

This is not your typical read-once-and-set-aside book. It is designed to engage you in the process of learning and personal development. Draw the following samples to compare your current ability level to where you want to be in 5 weeks.

There is no right or wrong way to do things. Allow each image to sink in before letting your imagination guide your pencil. Your goal should be to capture each image as you perceive it and to express your unique perspective.

When you've finished the book, take a time to reflect on your journey. Return to the images you drew at the start and redraw them. Contrast your old drawings with your new ones. Take note of the changes, the subtleties you may have overlooked previously, and your growing confidence in your artistic expression.

It is vital to remember that perfection will not be attained immediately. . Remember that you can always go back and practice any concept you need to improve on. Rather than getting it right the first time, the goal is to learn how to be an artist.

TEST YOURSELF EXAMPLES

Draw A Circle

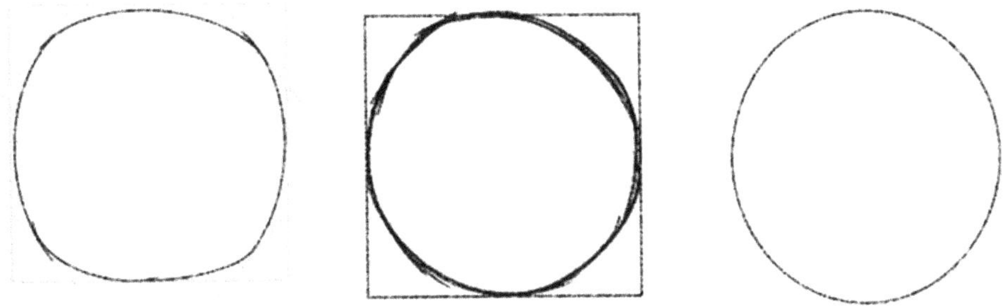

Draw a Frog

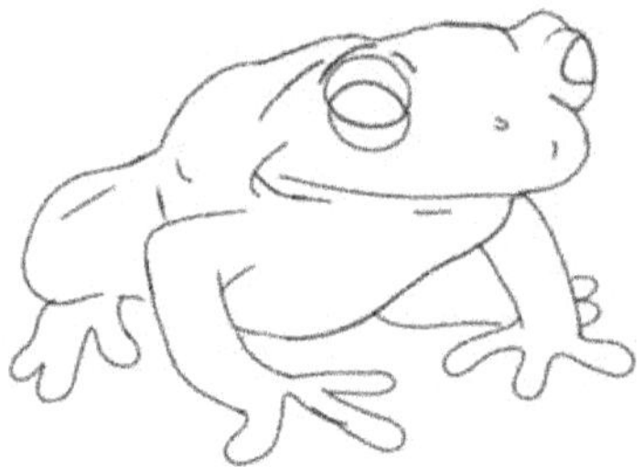

PART 1

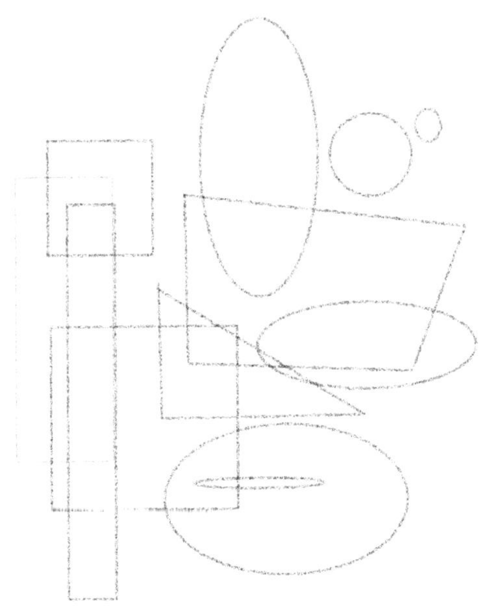

UNDERSTANDING THE BASIC SHAPES

This is the most fundamental concept for a beginner to grasp. Each of your sketches may be reduced down into simpler steps using only the most fundamental of shapes. Drawing anything complex can be difficult, but by first simplifying it into basic shapes, you can begin to represent its general structure.

We have all probably seen basic hapes like squares, rectangles, and circles before. However, most of the things we draw are made up of organic forms.

In this section, we will discuss how these complex organic structures can be reduced to their underlying geometrical building blocks.

As we walk you through this, we'll be discussing concepts like perspective and foreshadowing, so let's take a look at them now.

Things to Remember

- Learning to draw the square lays the groundwork for drawing cubes.
- All organic drawings have their origins from geometric shapes.
- Drawing a circle leads to the creation of ellipses, cylinders, balls, and other shapes. Truly, it's all connected.

Straight Lines

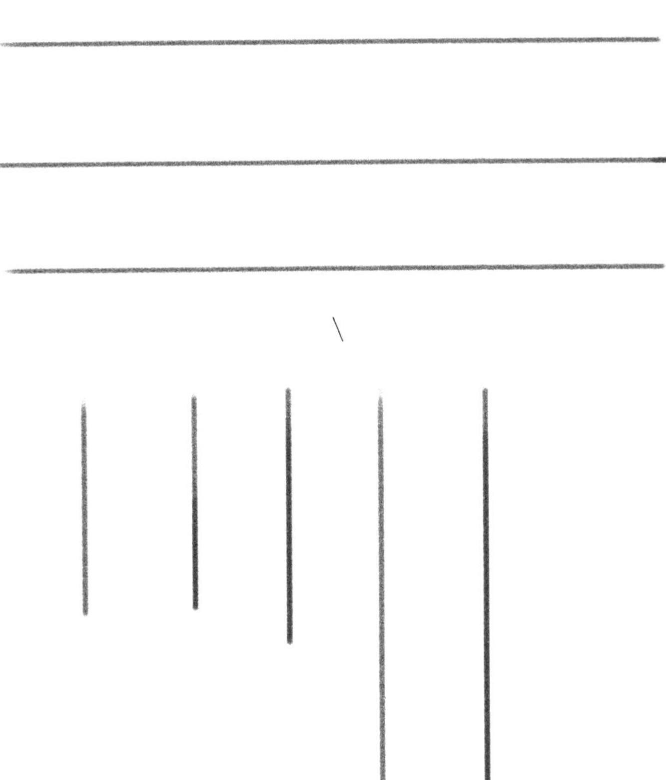

Long, fluid strokes should be used to sketch straight lines. You can improve your speed by practicing with a dot at each end of the line which you then try to connect to the other.

Circle

Start by drawing a medium-sized square with a ruler and writing A and B in the top left and right corners.

Then, draw straight lines from A to the other end of the square and call it "A." Then repeat the process with point b. Place the letters c and d on two lines in the middle.

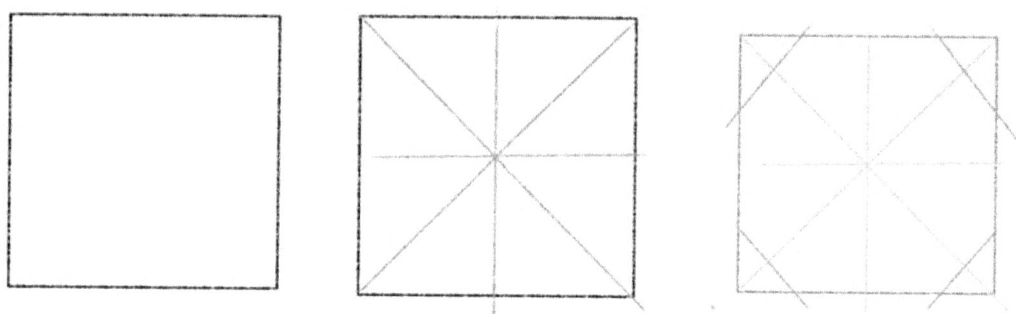

Get rid of the square sides and connect the points at the bottom. Keep working on it until it feels like it has a round shape. Then, get rid of any extra lines and make sure the circle is perfect.

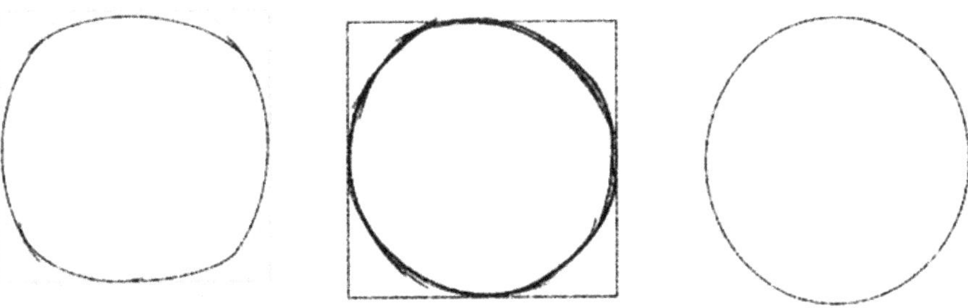

You can also try drawing a circle by hand and making changes as needed until it is perfectly round.

Drawing circles will help you get the hand-eye balance you need to make shapes that are accurate and have good proportions. Once you know how to draw circles well, you can use those skills to draw balls, watermelons, and other more difficult round shapes.

A Square

Four straight lines, two along the horizontal axis and two along the vertical axis, come together to make a basic square. It is pretty simple to draw.

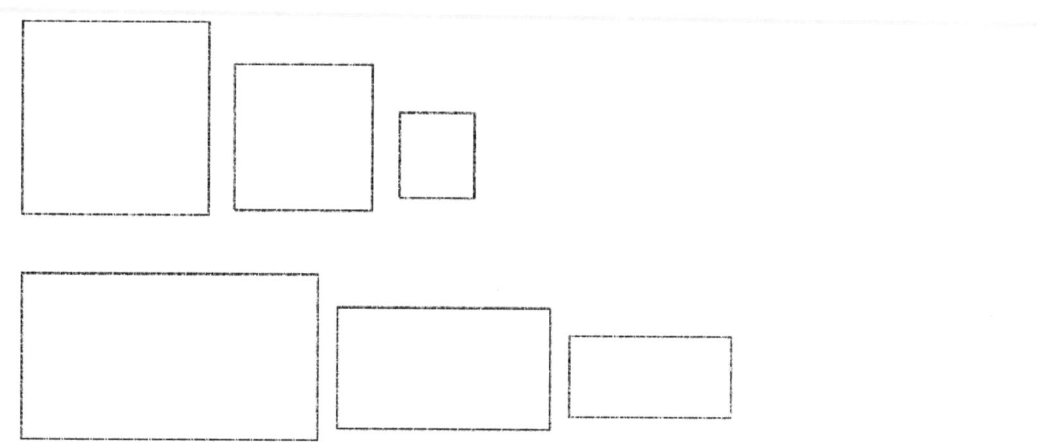

Start by drawing a few dots to show where the sides of the shape will meet. Put your pencil on the starting point, then take a deep breath and focus on where you want to end up. Just move your pencil along the imagined road and erase it when it gets to the end.

The Ellipse

An ellipse is a circle that has been tilted. Ellipses can be found in nature or man-made items, such as a bicycle wheel. Tires, toilet paper, and general openings that appear to have a circular opening. Even an empty soda can.

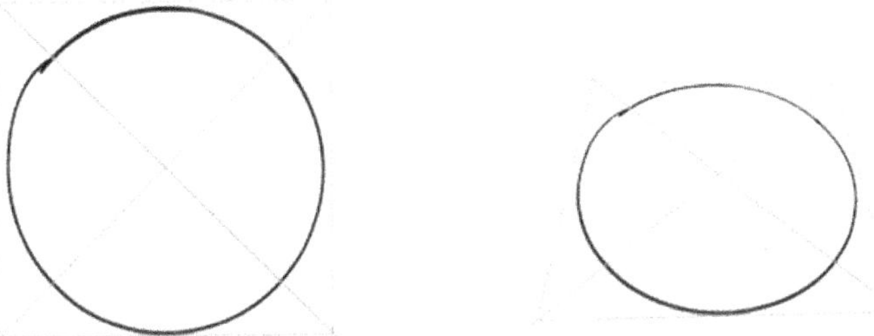

The shape of the hole hasn't changed, only where it is. By making an ellipse, you can show that change. When we move below eye level, the rim is also oval. So, an ellipse is just a circle seen from a different angle.

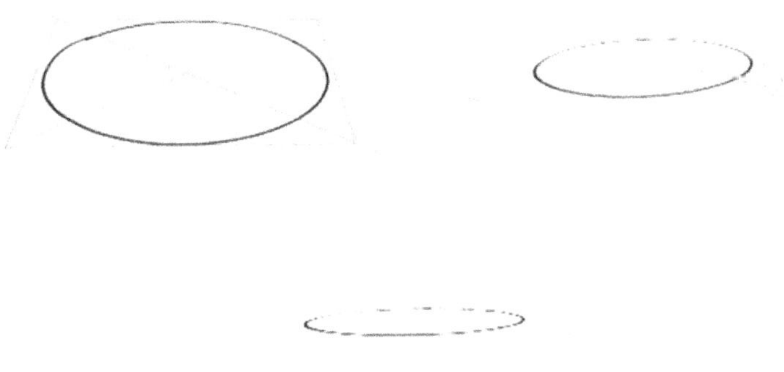

Eye level view

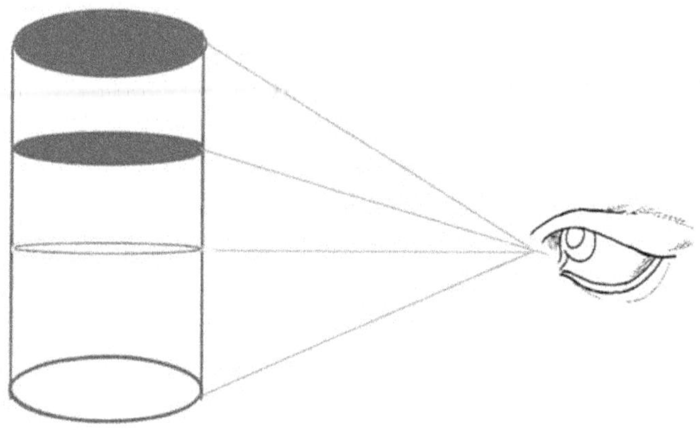

Various titled perspective of an elipse.

Let's look more closely at what an oval looks like. When we look straight down into a coffee cup, the hole looks like a circle. However, when we pick up the cup and hold it in front of us, the circle changes into an ellipse. When you hold it up to your eyes, it resembles a line. If we keep lifting it up, the bottom of the cup will look like a second circle.

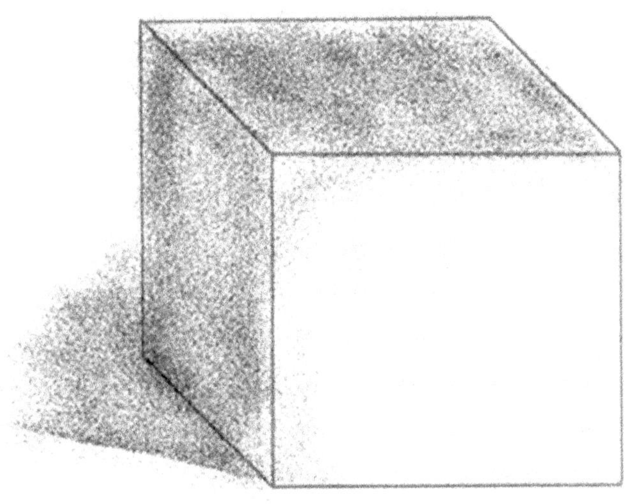

PART 2

HOW SHAPES CREATE FORMS

Forms are 3D things that have volume, depth, and weight. They are made by putting together shapes, shading, and highlighting methods. By starting with shapes and going on to forms slowly, you can learn how to draw and build a strong foundation for your skills.

A Cube

A cube is a square that has three sides. Depending on where you put the cube, you can see two or three sides.

To make a cube, you need to:

• Draw a square.

• Make a second square that overlaps the first one and is a little higher and to the side.

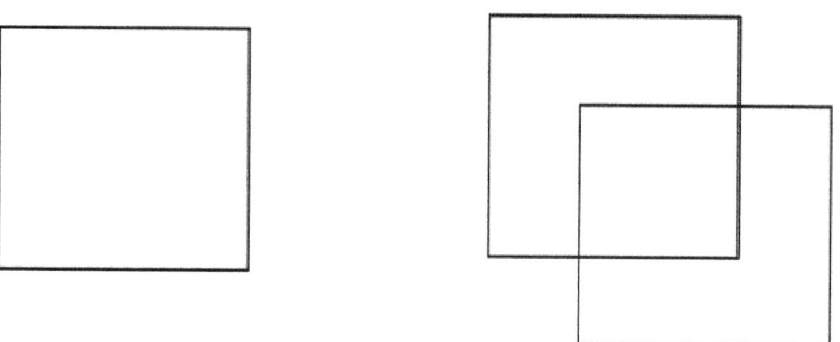

- Connect the four corners of the square.
- Remove the inside lines

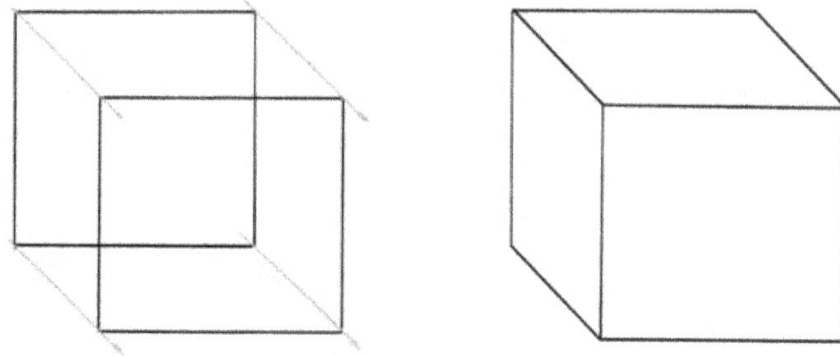

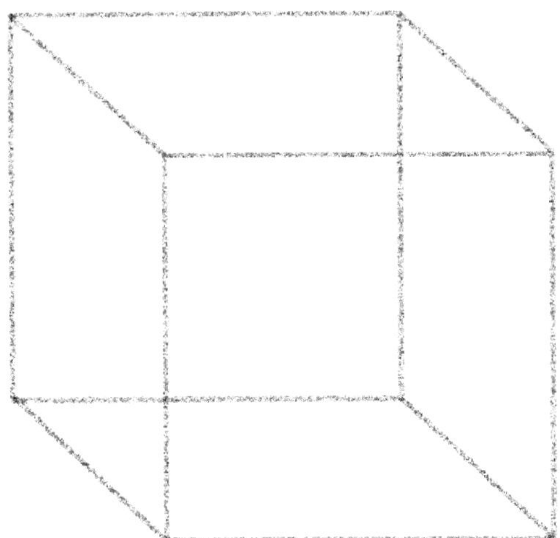

From CUBES to DICES

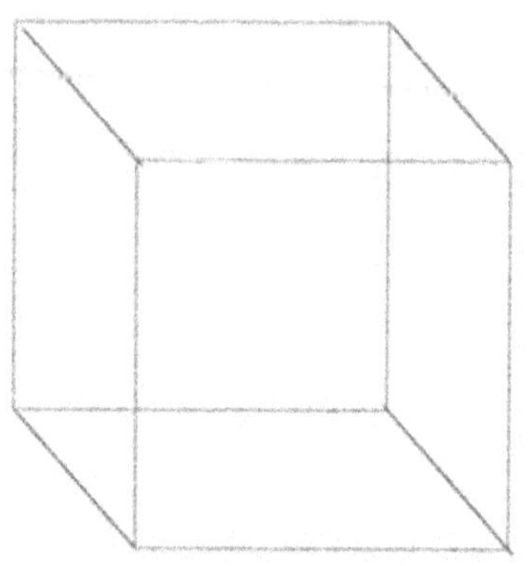
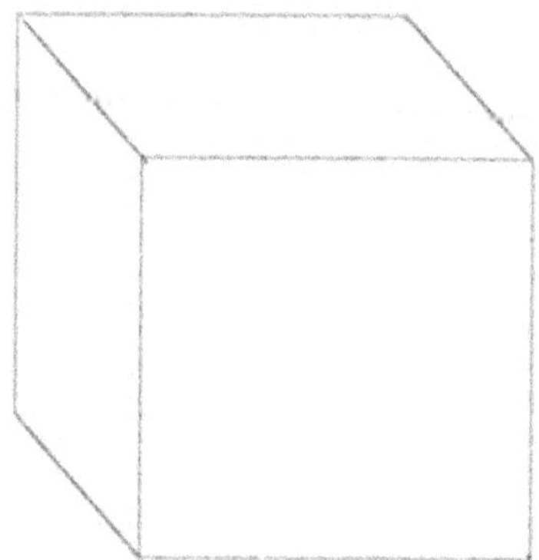

Draw a square and then create a second square that overlaps the first one and is a little higher and to the side.

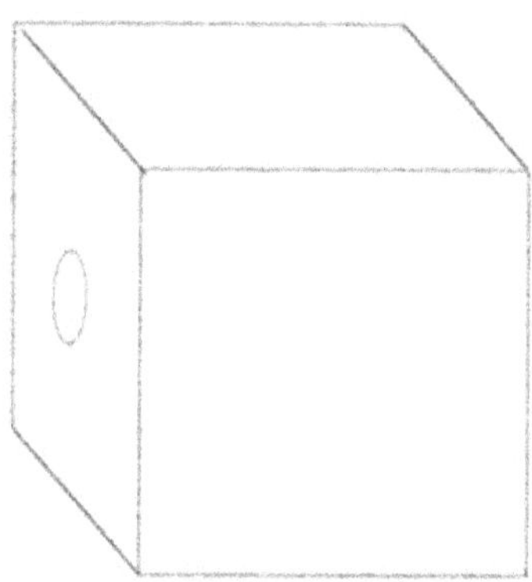
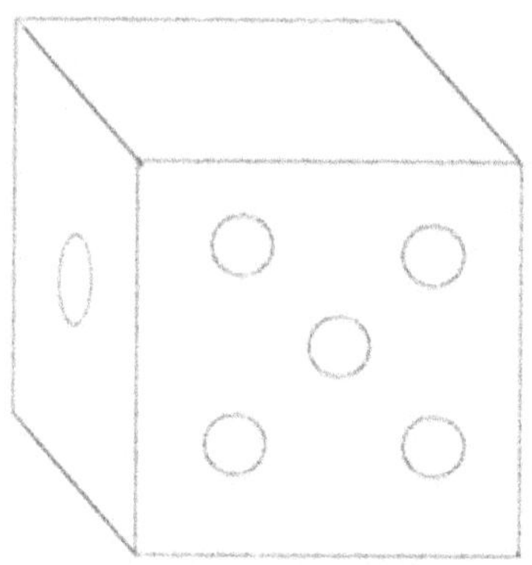

Draw a square and then create a second square that overlaps the first one and is a little higher and to the side.

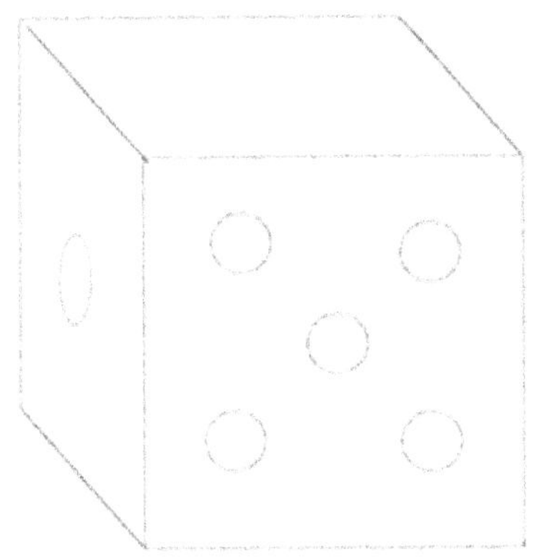

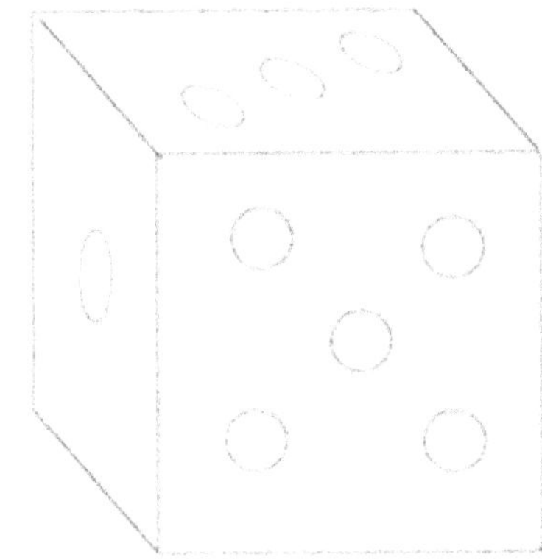

Connect the four corners of the square. Remove the inside lines

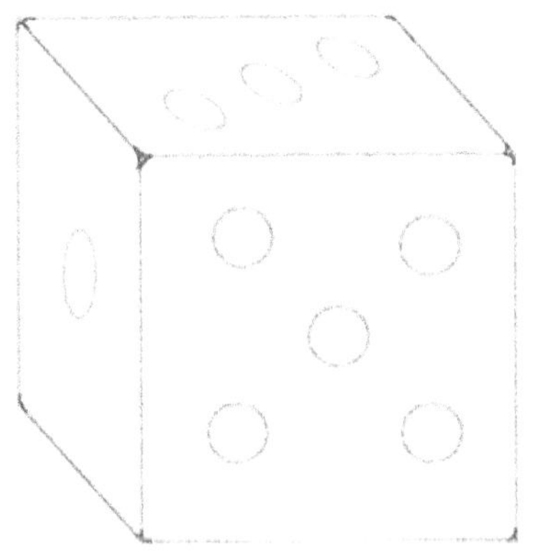

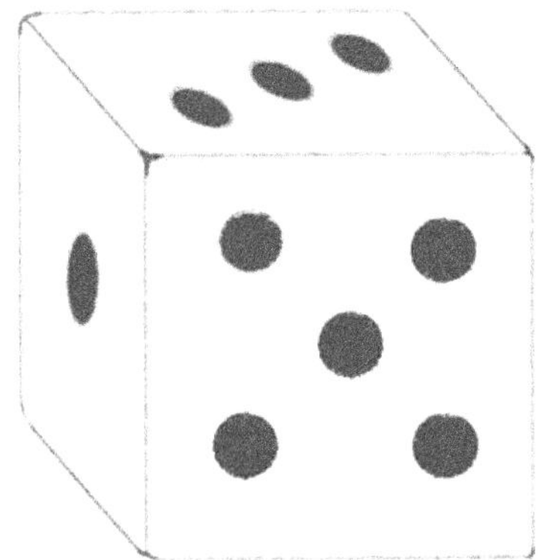

Begin to add the black circles and then shade them a dark circle

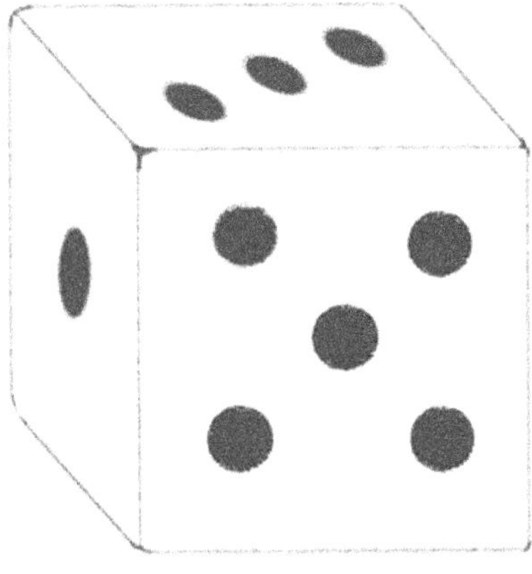

Erase any lines that appear not straight enough and redo them

MORE EXAMPLES

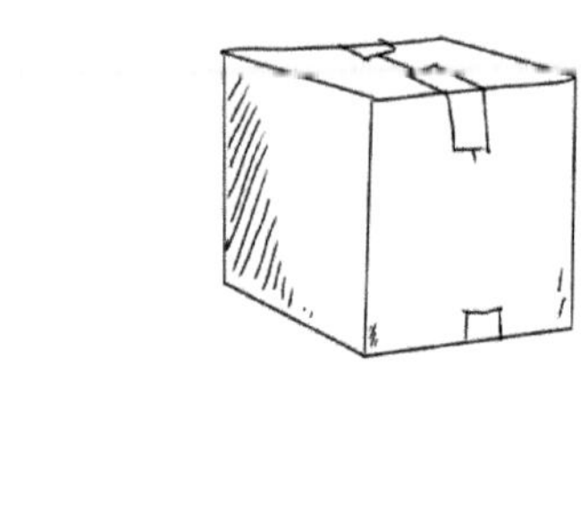

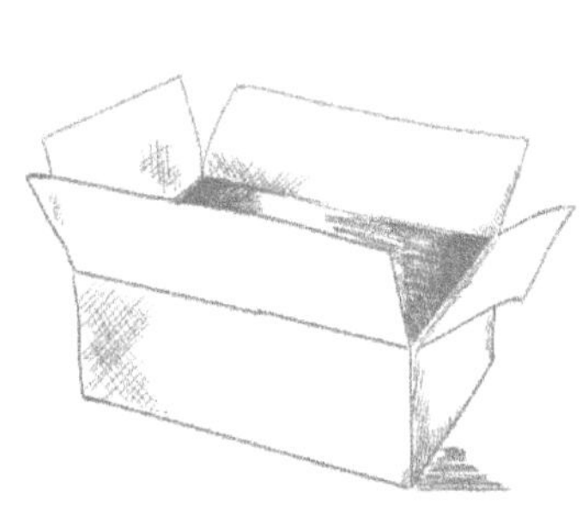

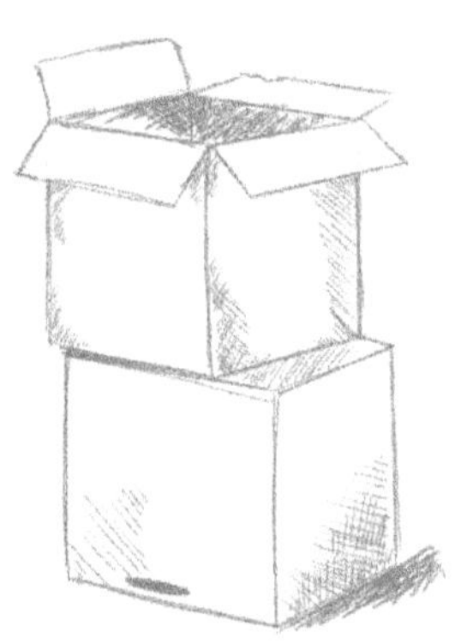

1. CUBES TO CARDBOARD BOXES

Continue with the same steps as mentioned earlier and then once your cube I completed, it's time to draw the handles.

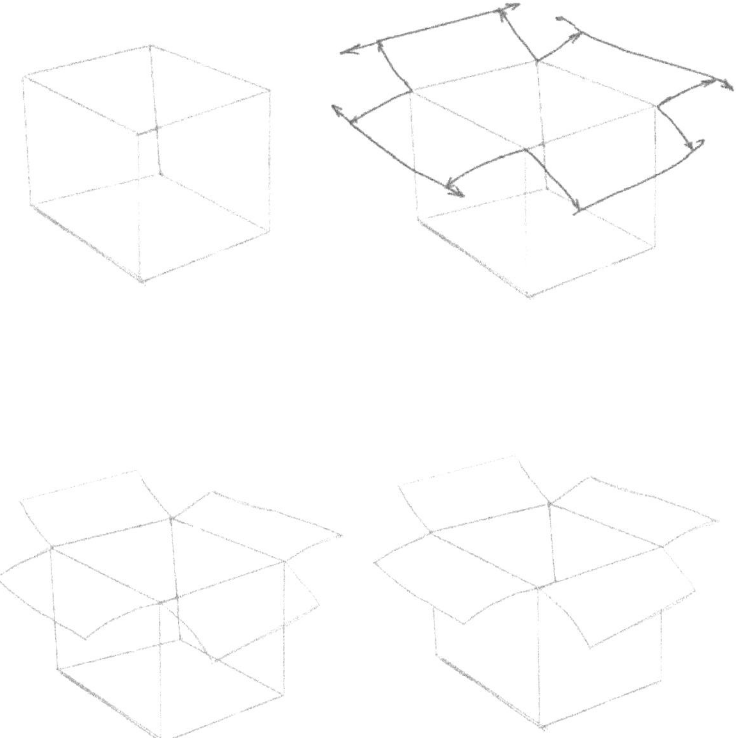

Draw squares to represent the handles, make sure some lines are curved.

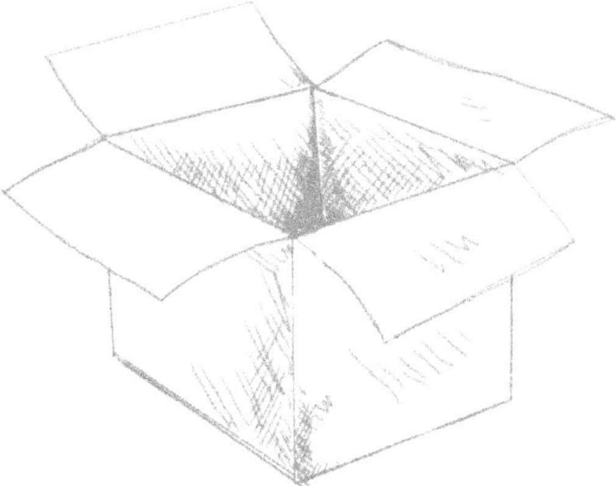

Next, begin to add more details by cross-hatching on the carton

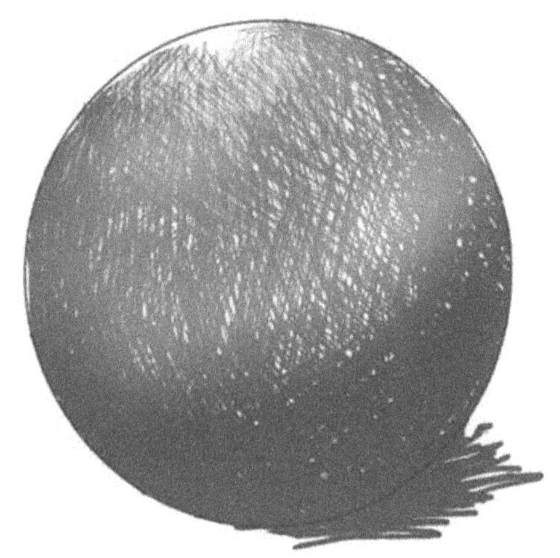

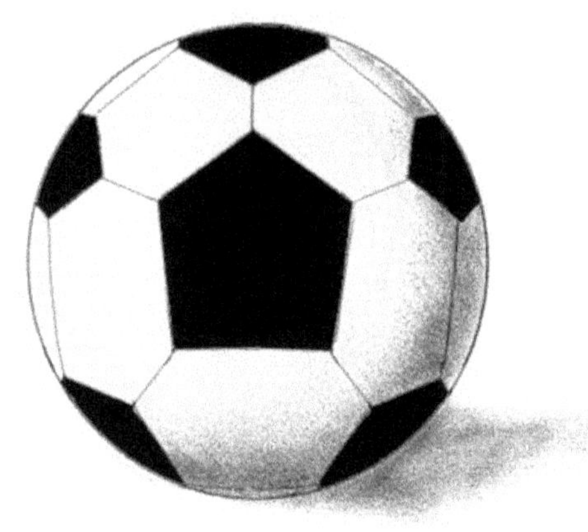

2. CIRCLES TO BALLS

You should learn how to draw a circle before you try to draw a ball. The basic form of a circle is used to make many round things and If you can draw circles well, you'll be able to understand and draw a ball's basic shape and size better.

Start with a circle

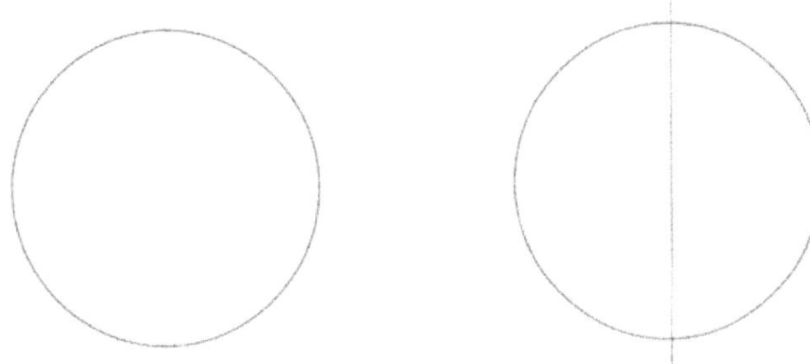

Draw a vertical line at the center of the circle, this is to help position the hexagon shape

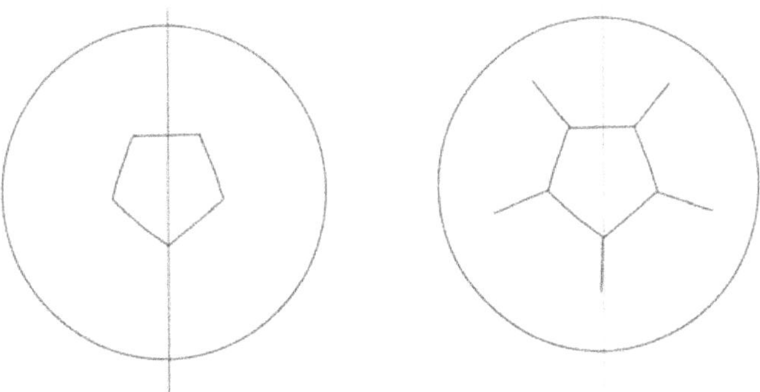

Add a hexagon shape at the center of the circle. Keep adding more shapes to your soccer ball until you fill out the circle.

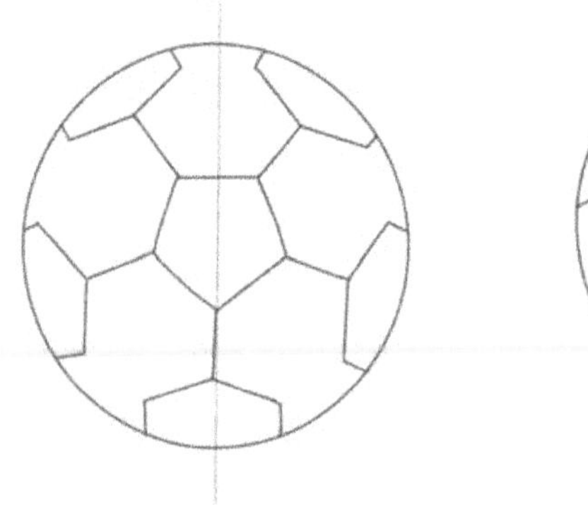

Colour in the hexagons in an alternating pattern

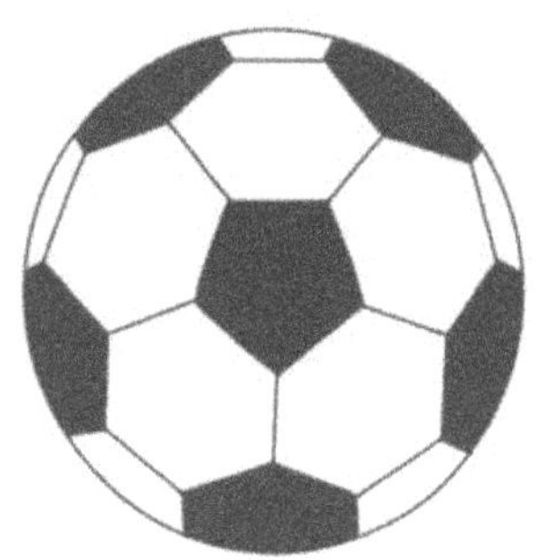

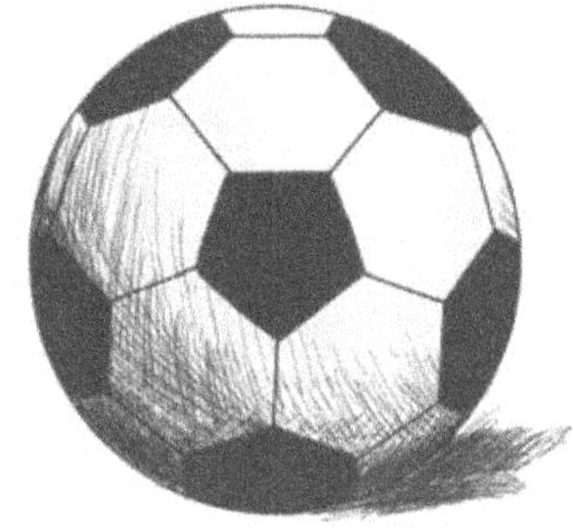

Begin to shade the ball, making enough space for the shadows.

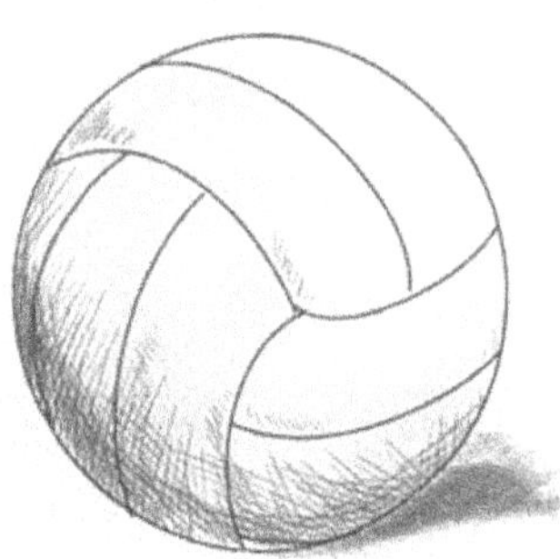

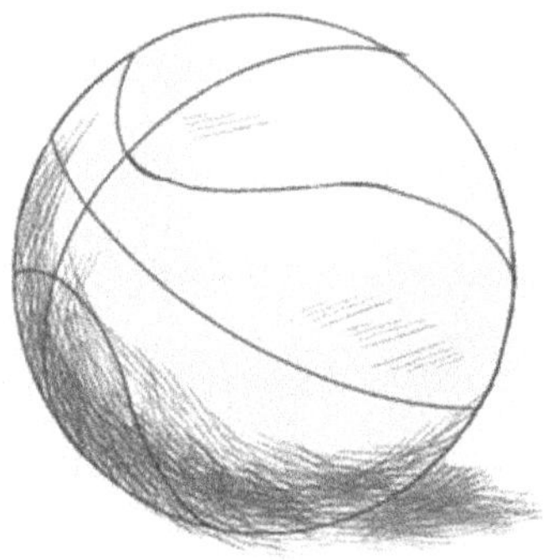

This technique can also be used for basketballs...

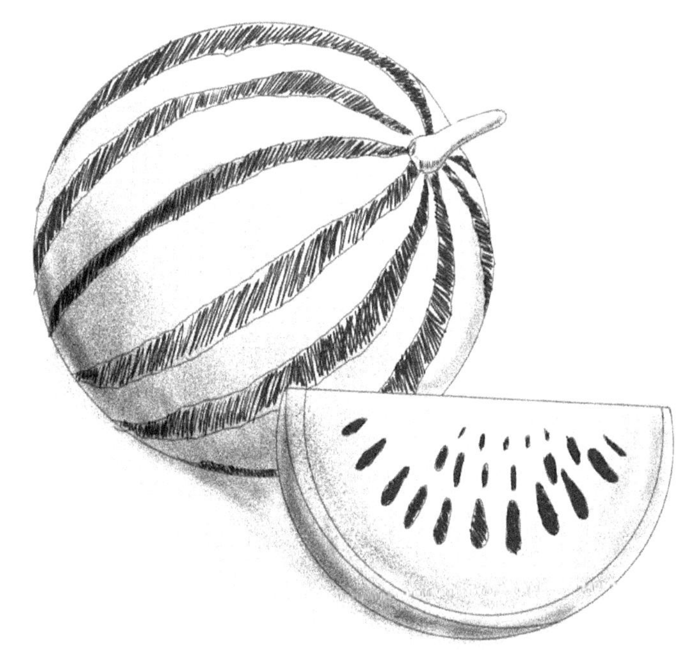

3. CIRCLES TO WATERMELONS

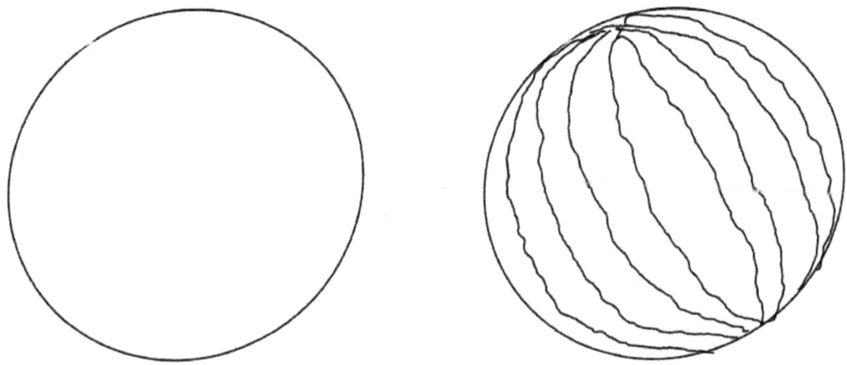

Draw a circle and then add a small curled line to the top of the circle

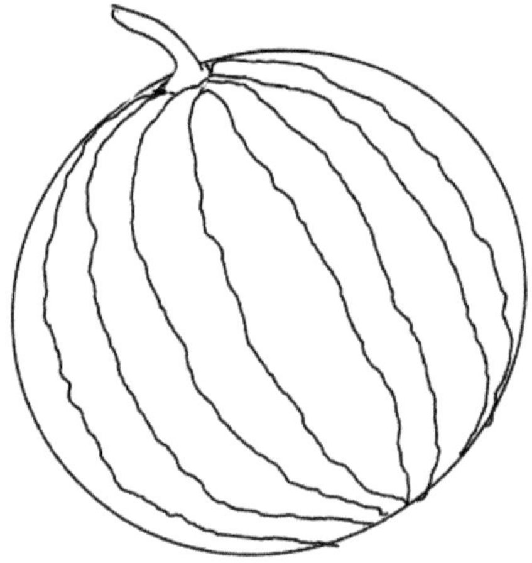

Add the stem by drawing a long, wavy line near the bent line you already drew

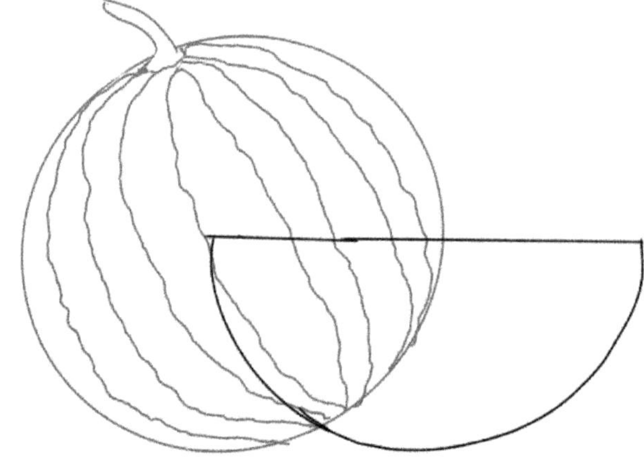

Draw the watermelon with half a circle, then add the rind and the edges.

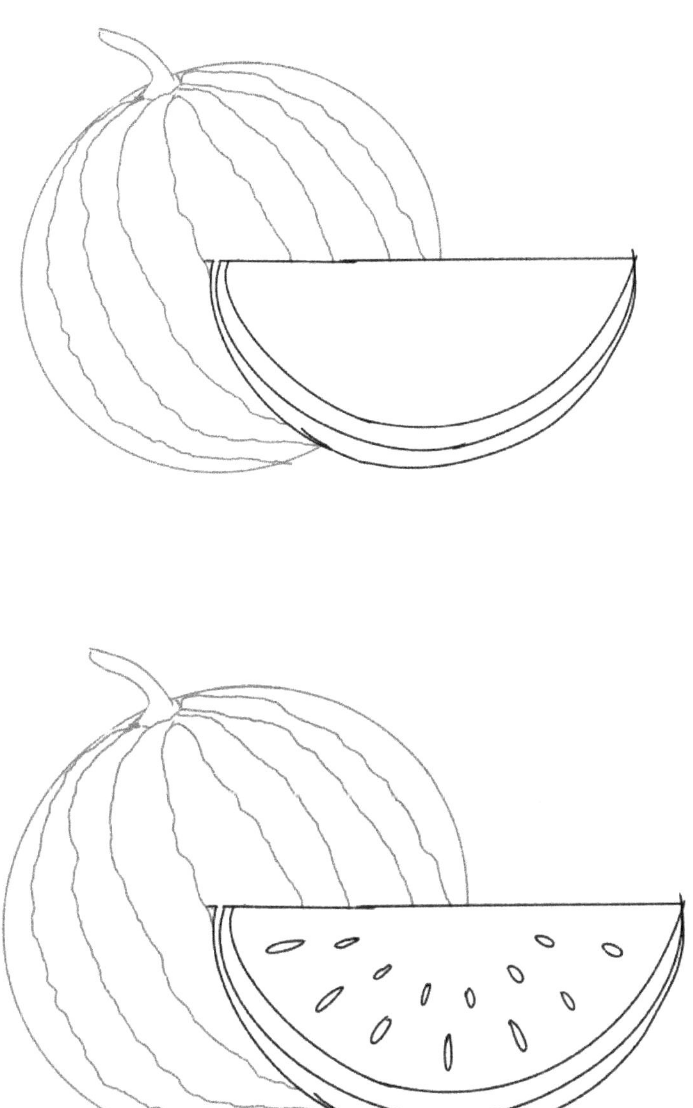

Inside the watermelon slices, draw small ovals to show the seeds. Focus on the top of the sliced watermelon as you draw a rough shape

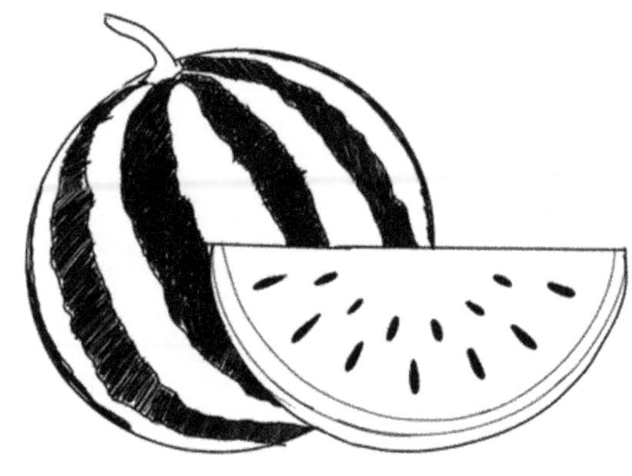

Use the eraser to get rid of any extra lines.

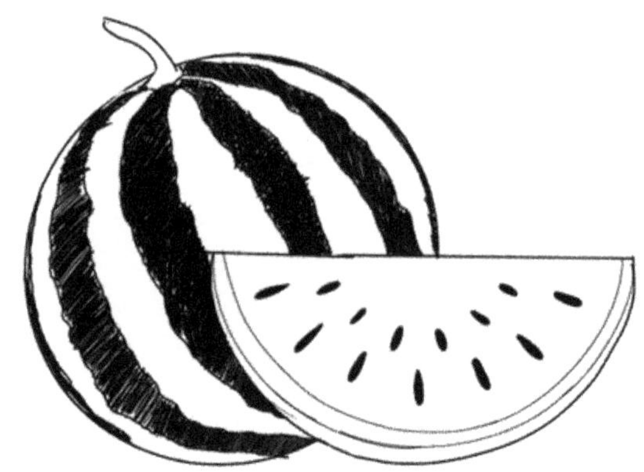

PART 2

LIGHTENING AND SHADING

If we want to make convincing images in our art, we need to be able to play with light, shadows, cast shadows, values, and other things.

Light Source

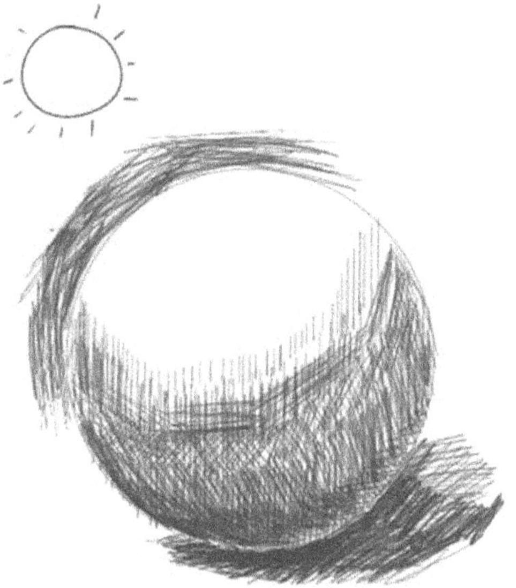

If you want to show depth in a way that looks real and realistic, you need to understand and draw the light source correctly. The light source determines where, how much, and what kind of light falls on your pictures. Use light, not a pencil, to make your images look like it has depth

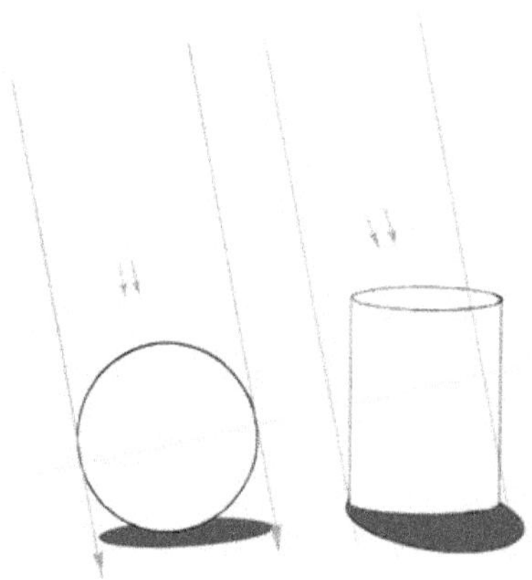

The light source comes from the left in the image above and in turn, the shadow cast is in the opposite direction.

Your source of light could be the sun, a window light, or a lamp. When there are more than one source of light, the bright and dark colors change and are harder to predict. For this lesson, I will only use one light source to make learning about light and shade easier. There are mainly two kinds of light sources:

• Direct light

• Refracted light

Direct light is any part of the form that gets light from the light source straight on. Reflected light, also called "bounced light," is light that hits the onto the form from nearby surfaces on the form's dark side. The shadow side of a sphere, for example, is faintly lighted by light bouncing off the floor and onto this side of the item. Because direct light can wash off local color, the color of the object is often most true in this area. Without reflected light, the viewer would only see the illuminated side, creating an unappealing image.

Shadows

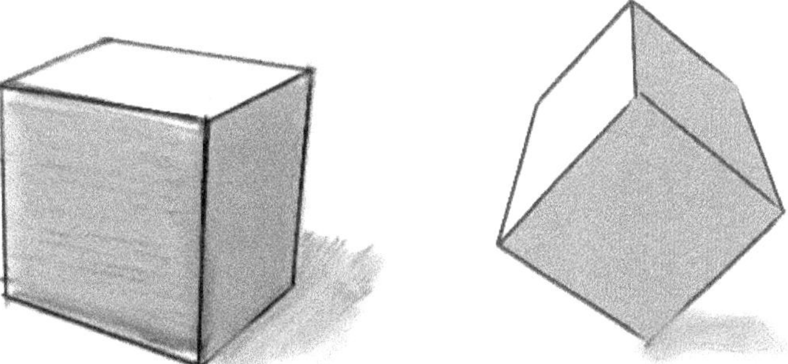

Because shadows are always a direct response to whatever the light touches, you must be able see what factors are at work before you can create the right representation of your image that accurately captures light and shadows.

Examine and evaluate the shadow's form. Usually, shadows take on the form of the object that casts them.

Value

The value of a color is how dark or light it is. Value is very important in art because we see and understand things based on how dark or bright they are.

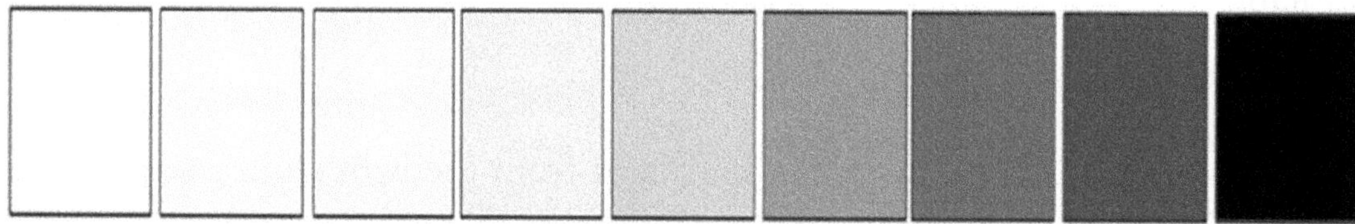

Not only is it important for drawing, Light is what makes everything we see and how we feel about our surroundings. When we can see something, it means that it is getting light from somewhere. As an item moves away from a source of light, less light can reach it, making it gradually darker. The thing goes into darkness, where light can't reach it anymore. This gives rise to a range of values.

SAMPLE LIGHT SOURCE AND SHADOW IN A PYRAMID

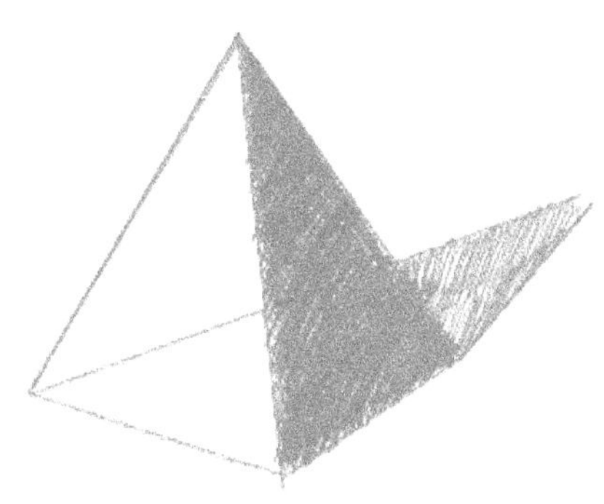

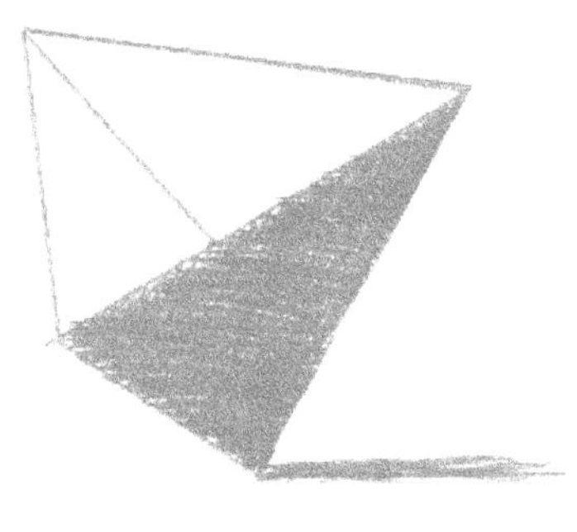

The source of light, the shape of the object, and the surface on which they are cast all influence shadows. If a single light strikes a cube, it will throw a square shadow; if a single light strikes a sphere, it will cast an elliptical shadow.

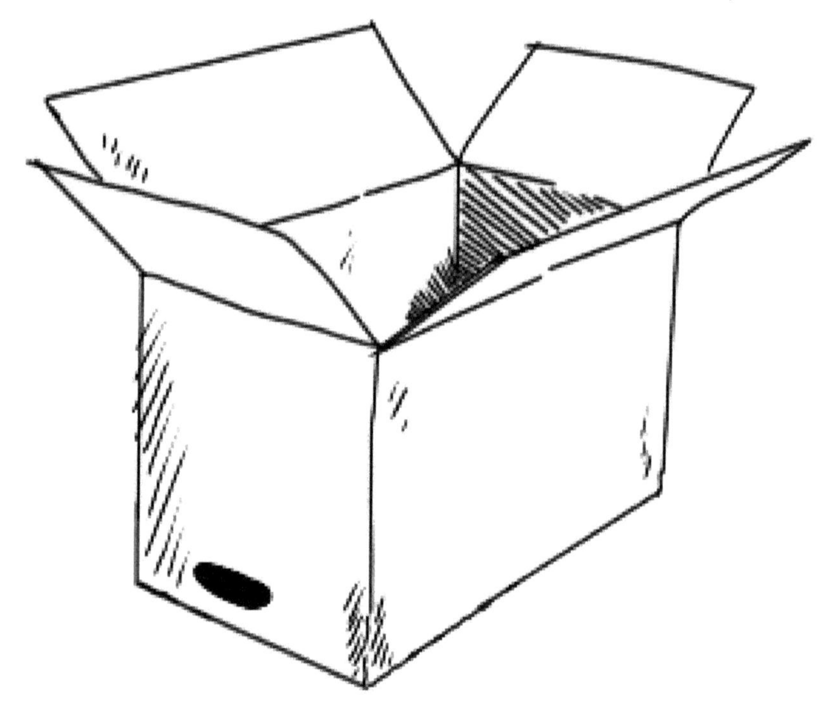

HATCHING AND CROSSHATCHING

Hatching and cross hatching are two ways to draw lines that can be used to create texture, value, and the sense of form and light. The most important tools for adding value and texture to a drawing are hatching and crosshatching. Drawings use simple lines in different patterns and densities to give a strong feeling of depth and realism.

Hatching

Hatching is made when lines are used to show the value of something on or around it. When hatching is used, most of the lines go in the same way and are parallel to each other.

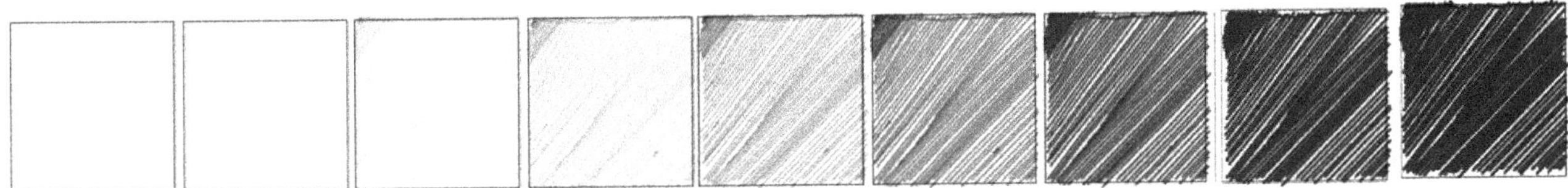

Cross Hatching

When cross hatching is used, the artist may start by adding value with hatching, but then let the lines cross over each other. The number gets darker the more the lines cross over each other.

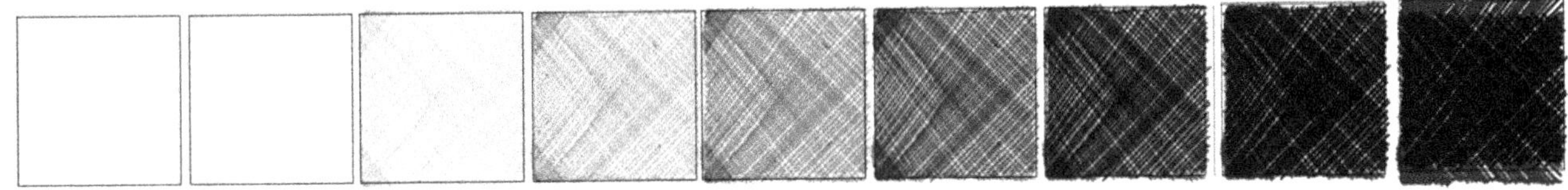

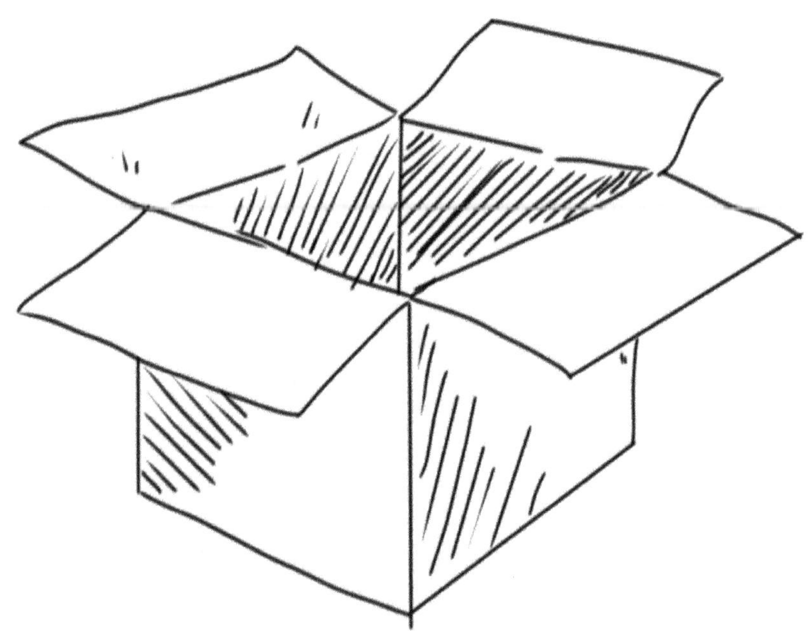

An example of hatching

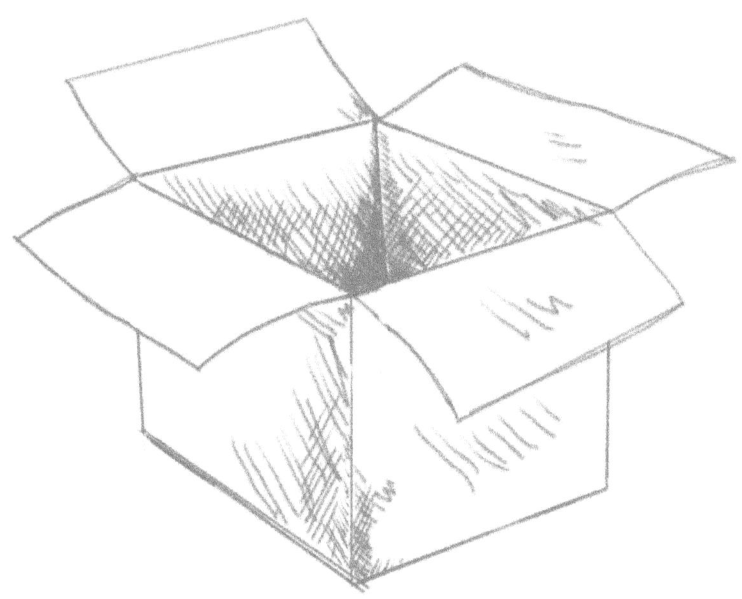

An example of Cross- hatching

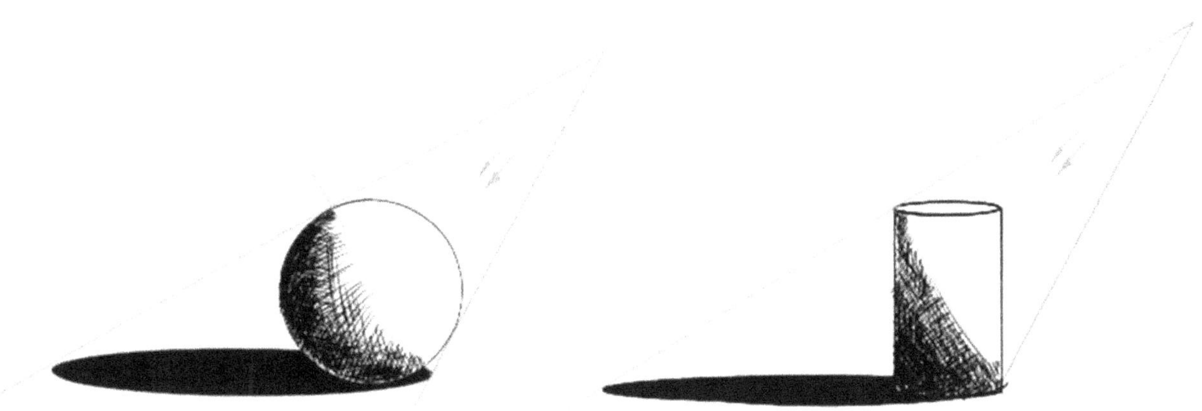

"That really puts things into perspective."

PERSPECTIVES

Perspective is a way to talk about how things get smaller or closer to the watcher as they get farther away. Perspective is an important part of almost all drawings, sketches, and paintings.

Perspective in art is what makes a picture or sketch look three-dimensional instead of flat. It's pretty simple, and you probably already know it but haven't used it in your work yet.

It's one of the rules you need to understand if you want to draw realistic and believable art. Learning how to use perspective and values to give your picture or drawing depth will make it look much more real.

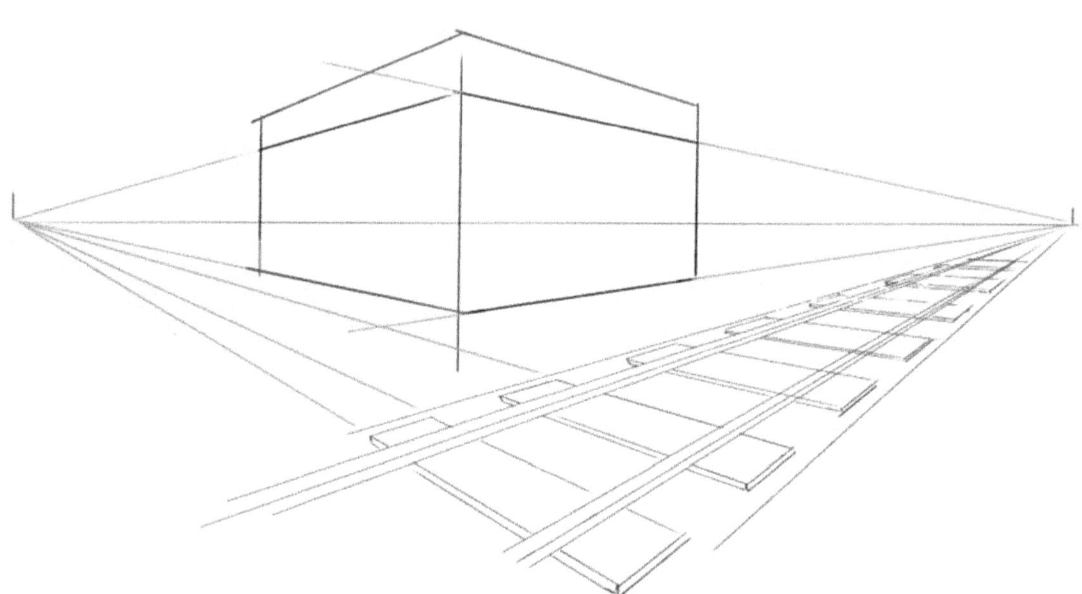

Terms to Note

Here is a list of phrases that are commonly used while discussing a one-point perspective drawing.

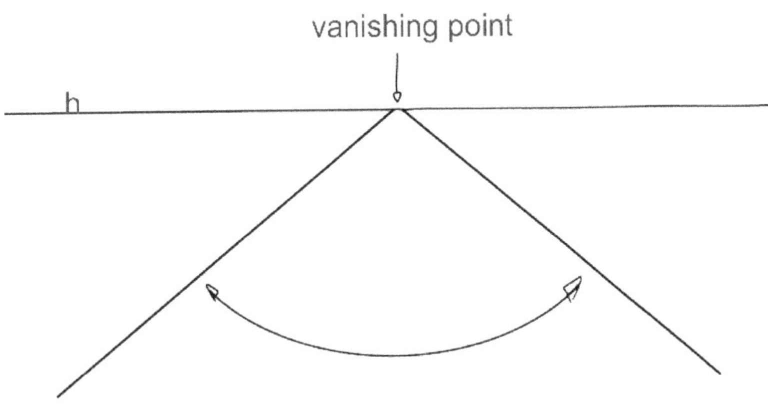

Viewpoint

A viewpoint is where you are when you look at your scene. A typical point of view is to look at a scene or item from eye level. The picture above shows how a person standing still and looking ahead at a road would see it.

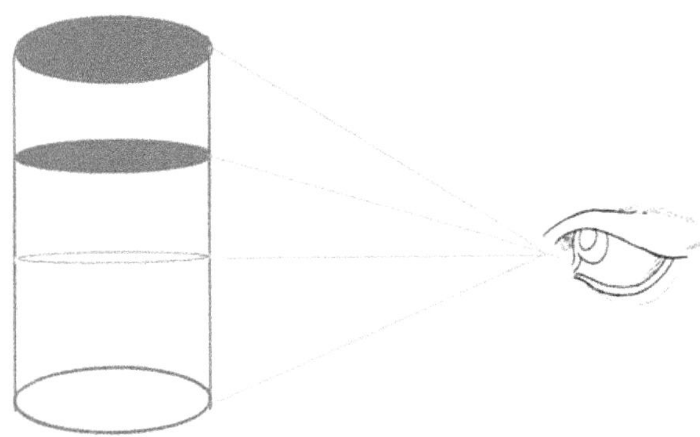

When you have a low viewpoint, you look at your subject from below, like when you look up to a window. A high viewpoint is looking down on something, like from a high rock at a beach below.

Horizon Line (H)

Eye level is an imagined line that is straight and far away. If you stand on a beach and look out into the ocean, the horizon line is easy to see. The horizon line is where the sky and the sea meet.

Vanishing Lines

Not the same as the vanishing point, this is when lines seem to meet up in the distance. The vanishing point is where all of these lines meet.

Orthogonal lines

Lines that give the illusion of more depth than there really is. They help you show that things in the distance look smaller and farther away. Some items that have orthogonal lines are roads or train tracks that go on for a long way. The road's sides would be like straight lines. At the bottom of your drawing, they are far apart, but as you get closer to the sky, they get closer together. With these lines, it looks like the road is going far away from you.

Horizontal lines are made so that they go from side to side along the sky.

Vertical lines are lines that go straight to the sky and go up and down.

One Point-Perspective

One-point perspective is often used to draw buildings, cityscapes, and other pictures with straight or square-shaped objects. It gives your pictures a sense of depth, distance, and realism by copying how things look in real life when seen from a certain point of view.

Notice how the train tracks get smaller and farther away as they go on?

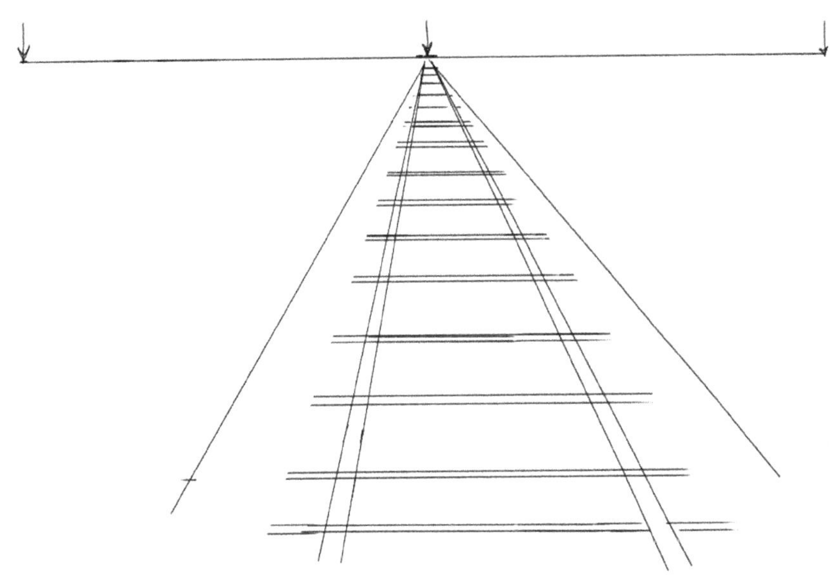

A railway track

Two-Point Perspective

People often use two-point perspective to draw cityscapes, interiors, and scenes with square or rectangular objects. It gives your drawings depth and reality by showing how things look when seen from different angles in real life.

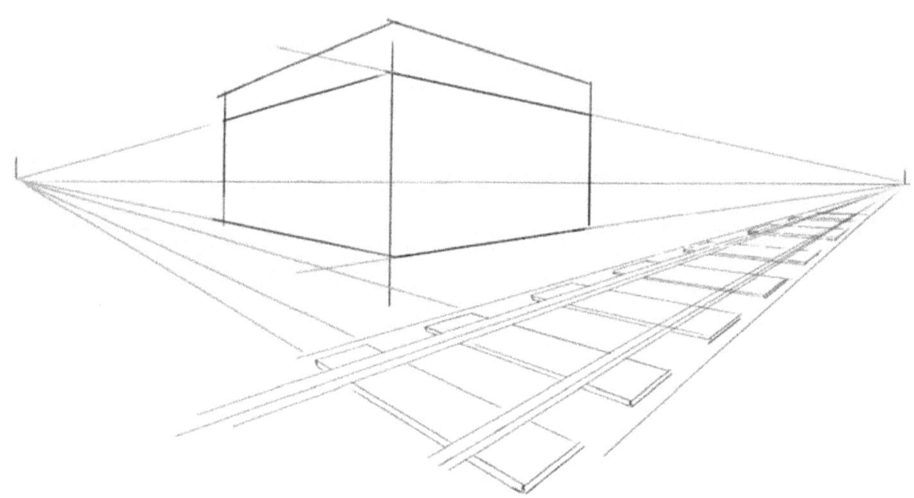

Two-point perspective drawing: This picture is a great example of a two-point perspective drawing because it shows both the side of the house and the railroad track.

Knowing Various Perspectives

Now that you know how to draw the basics, here's a fun step-by-step guide to drawing in perspective, which uses the power of illusion. It's one of the rules you need to understand if you want to write realistic and believable stories. Learn how to give your picture or drawing more depth by adding perspective and reducing the size of the apples as they move further.

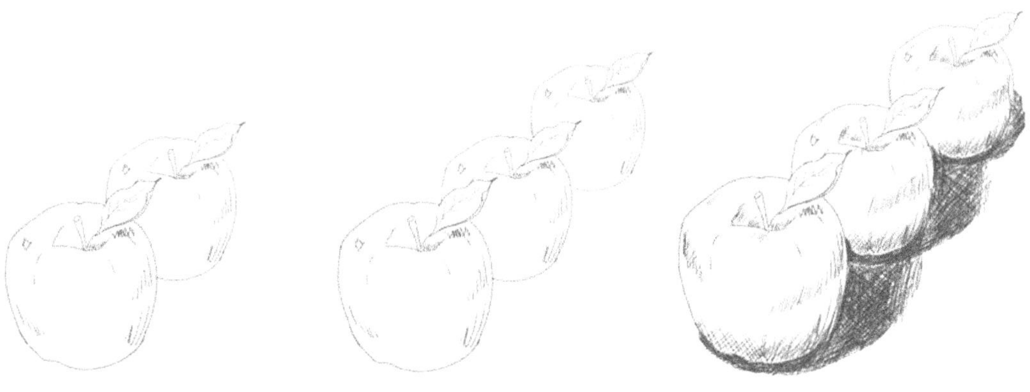

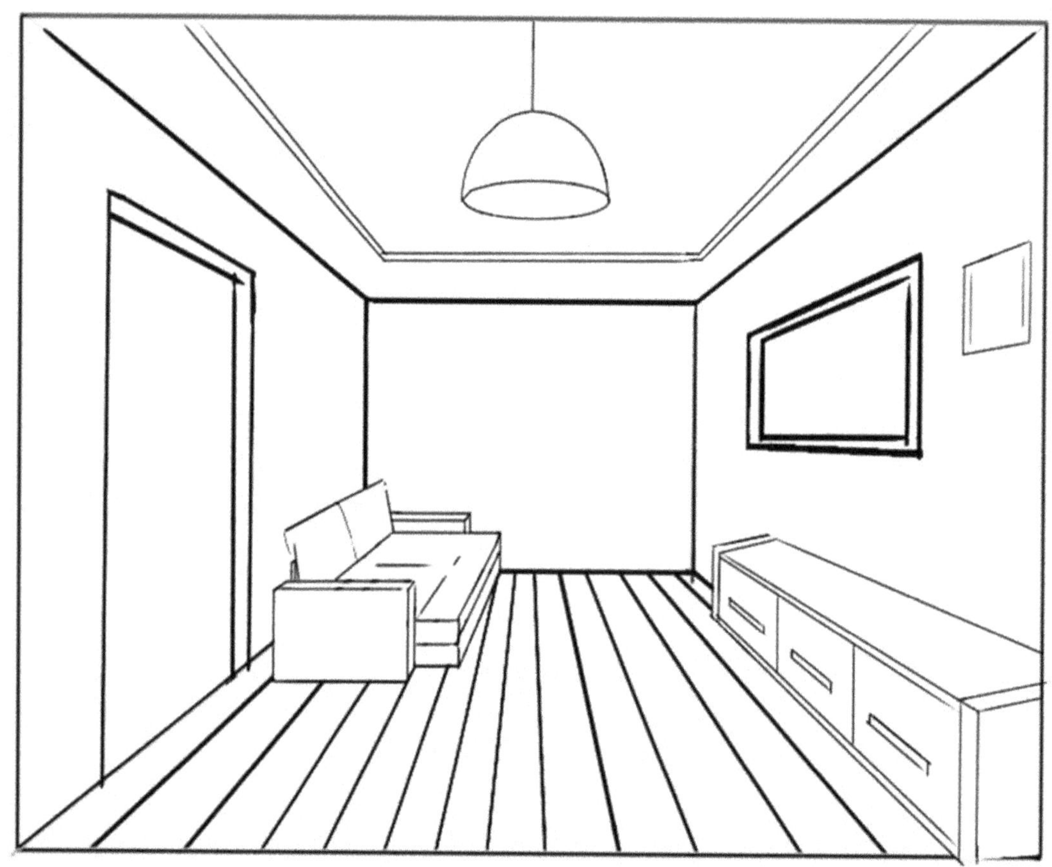

ONE POINT PERSPECTIVE DRAWINGS

By using one-point perspective, you can make cool drawings that look real and show how things get smaller as they get farther away. Have fun trying this method out and getting better at it.

A Room in One Point Perspective

Draw a big box or square and then cross it with two vertical lines.

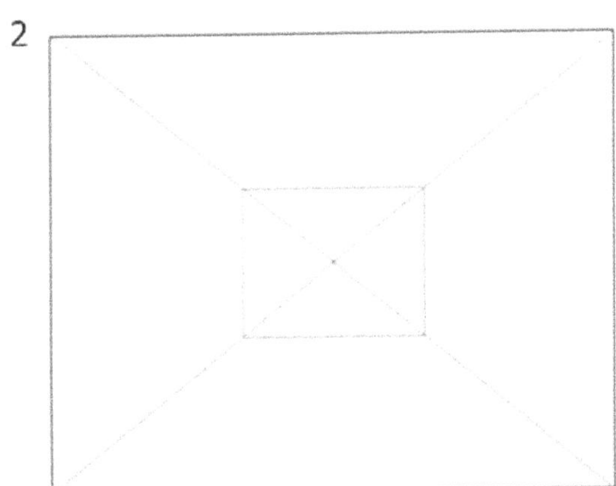

Make a smaller square in the middle of the intersecting line.

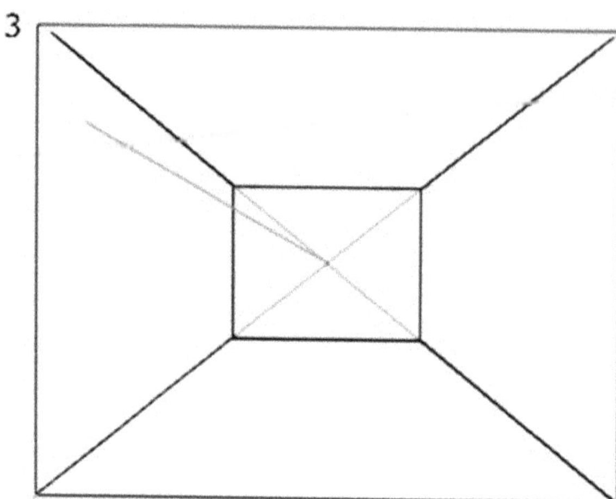

From the point where the room ends, start drawing the room's highlights. The door, picture frame, and floors are good places to start

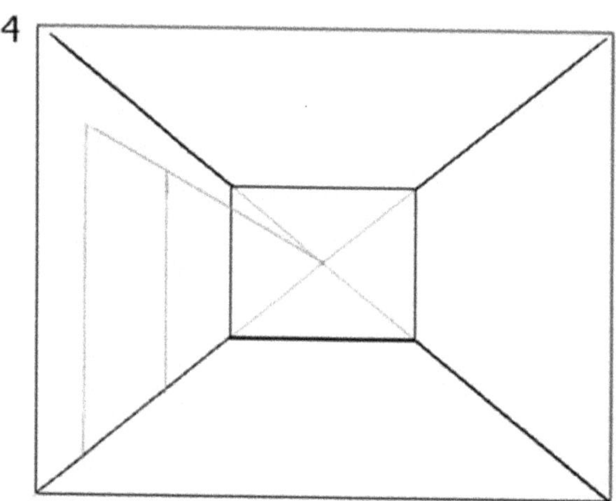

5

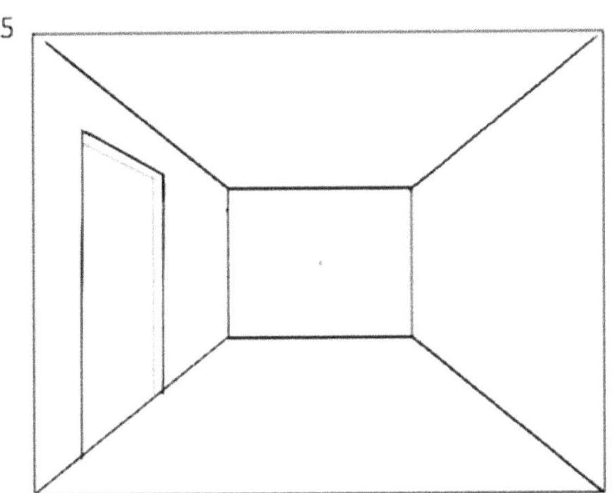

6

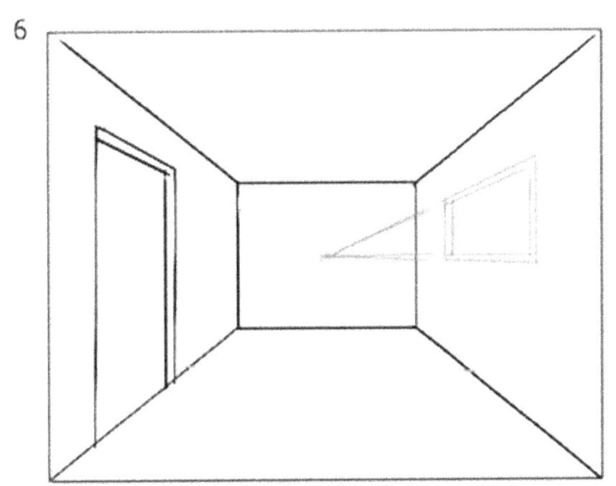

7

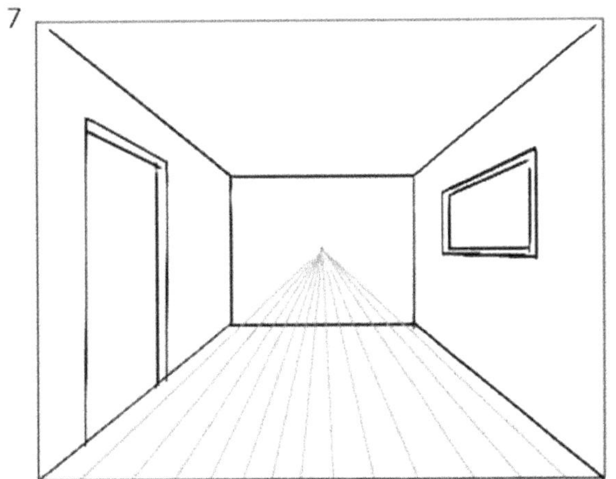

8

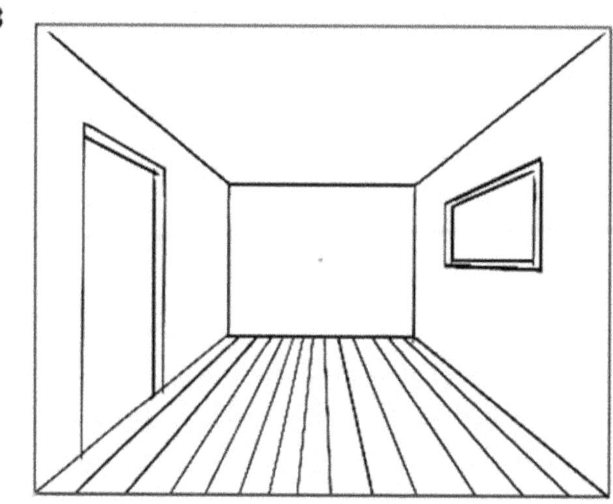

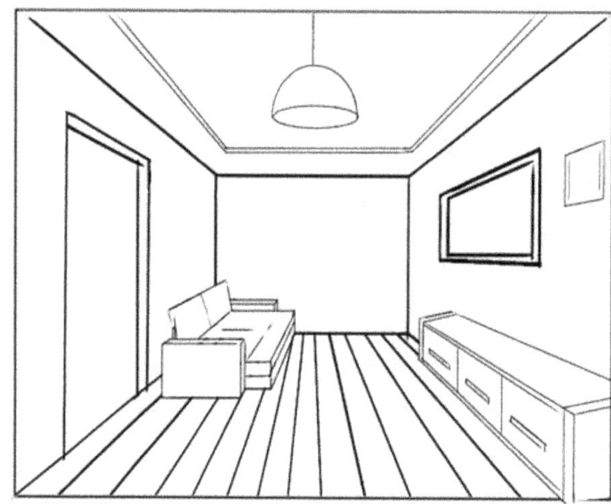

Start by drawing a thin line in the middle of the living room. Then, add furniture like chairs, TVs, and flower vases one at a time. Erase the lines that show the structure, and you're done.

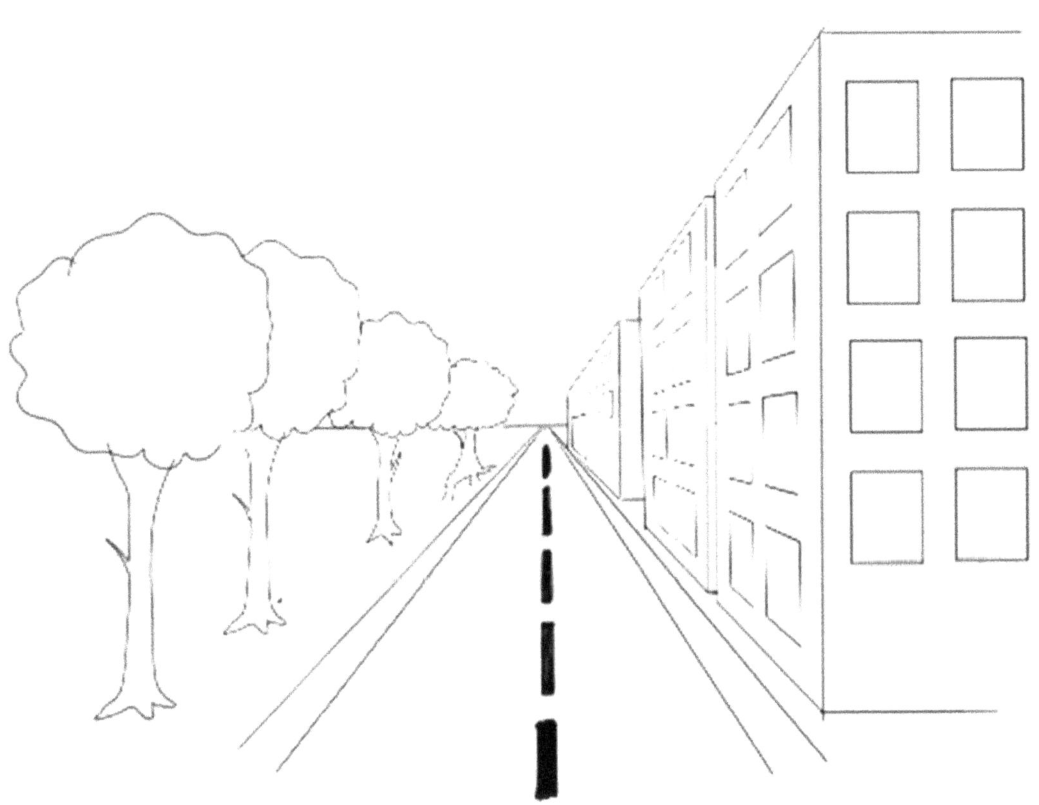

A CITY IN ONE POINT PERSPECTIVE

Even though it might look hard, drawing a city from one point of view is not hard. This is how;

Make a horizontal line with a point in the center.

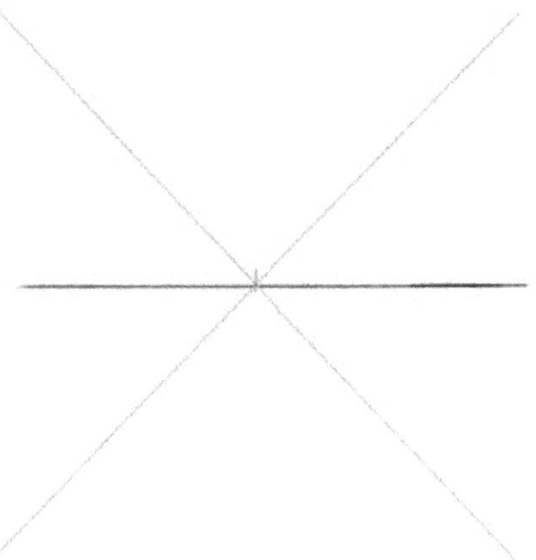

Draw guide lines to position the buildings and the road

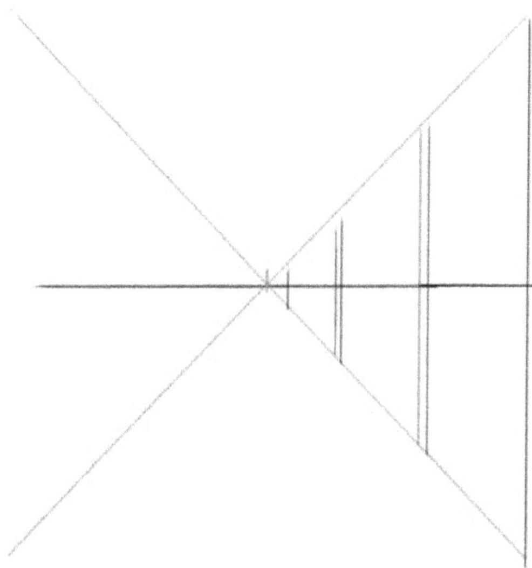

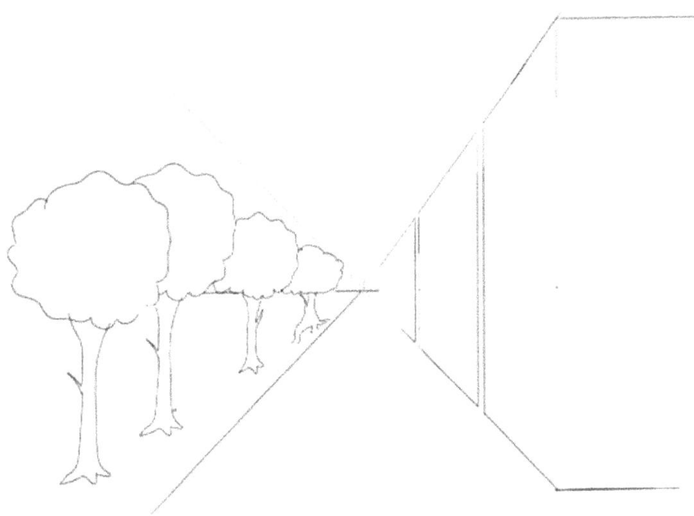

Remove the structural lines and start adding features like the outlines of the trees and square frames for the windows

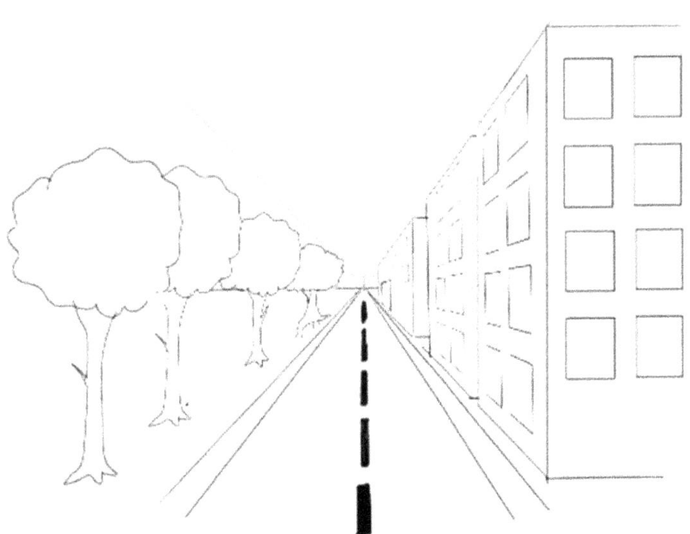

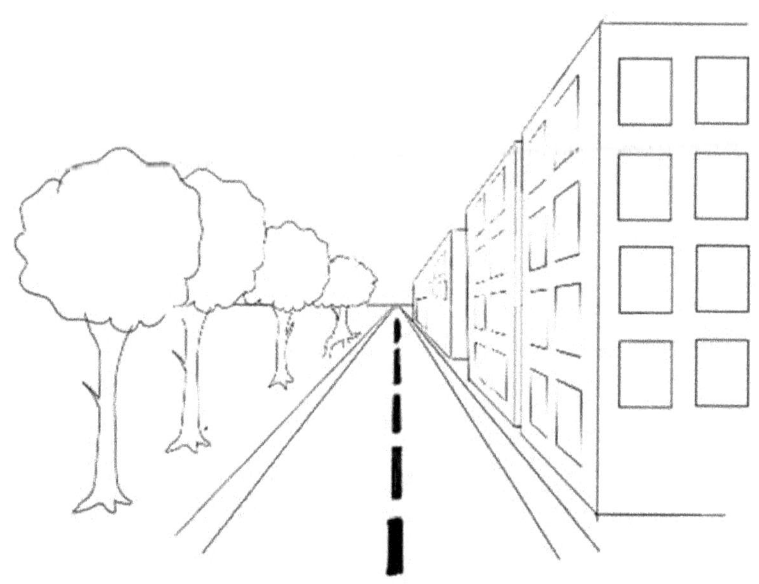

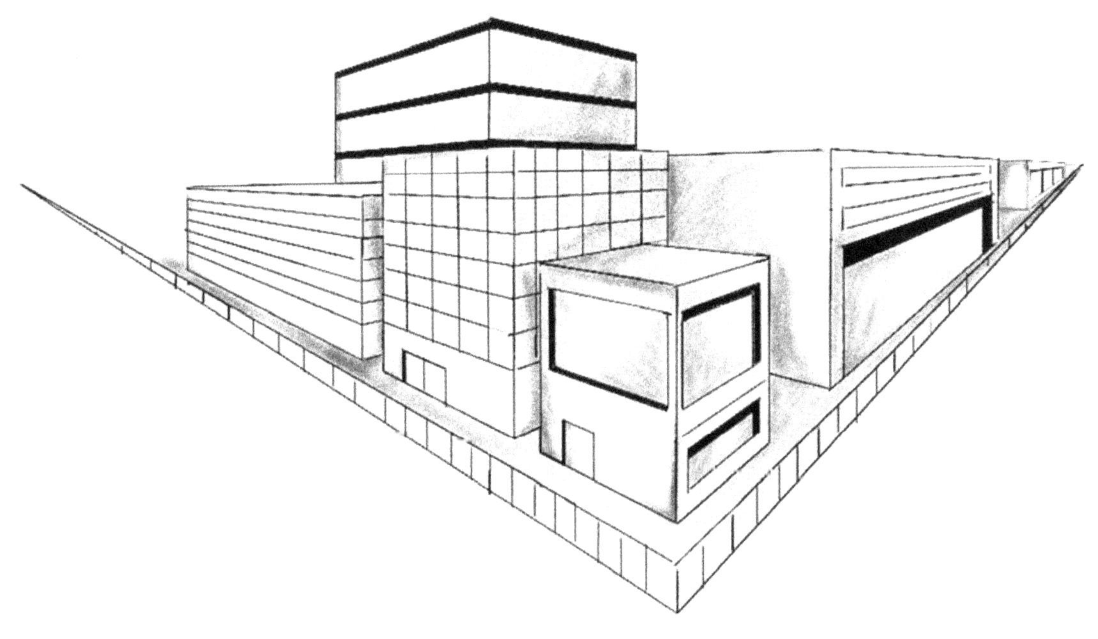

2 POINT PERSPECTIVE CITY

Draw a horizon line then draw a vertical line that meets with the horizon line at a 90 degree angle.

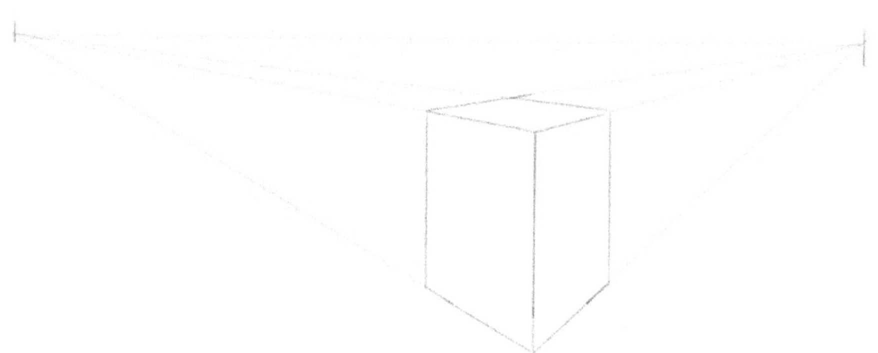

Draw a cube for the top of the building, then add more details, repeat the process until you have another

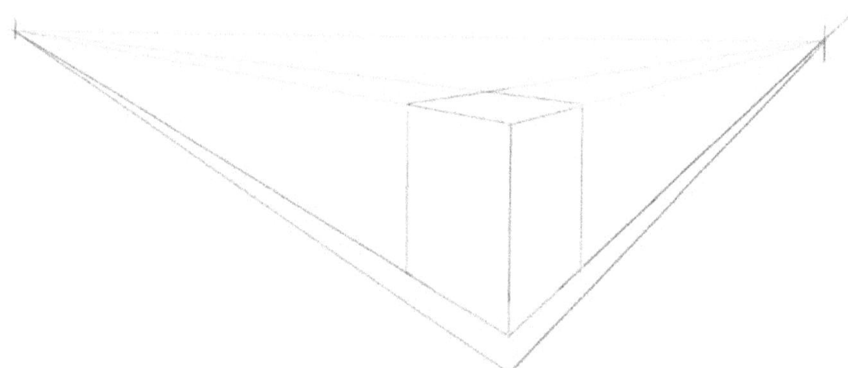

building.

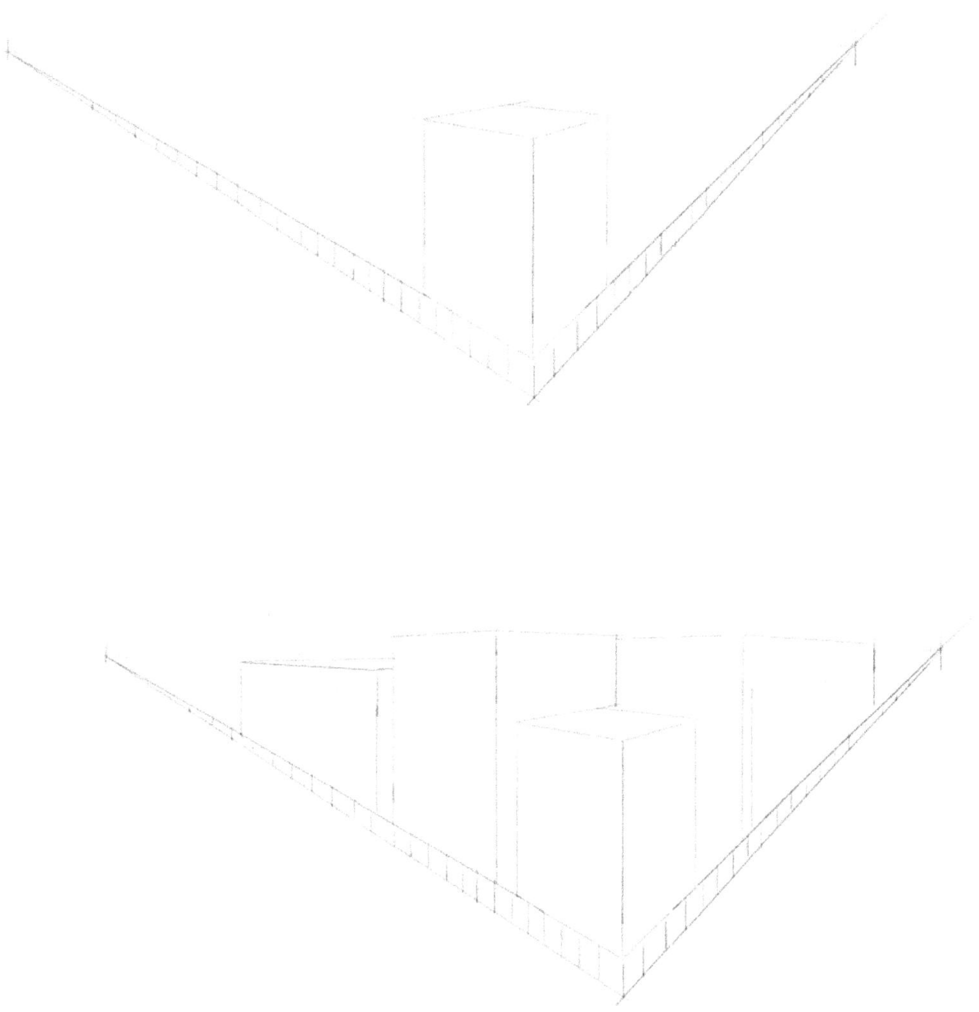

Draw a vertical line to define the midpoint of the next building. Then connect two diagonal lines to the vanishing point

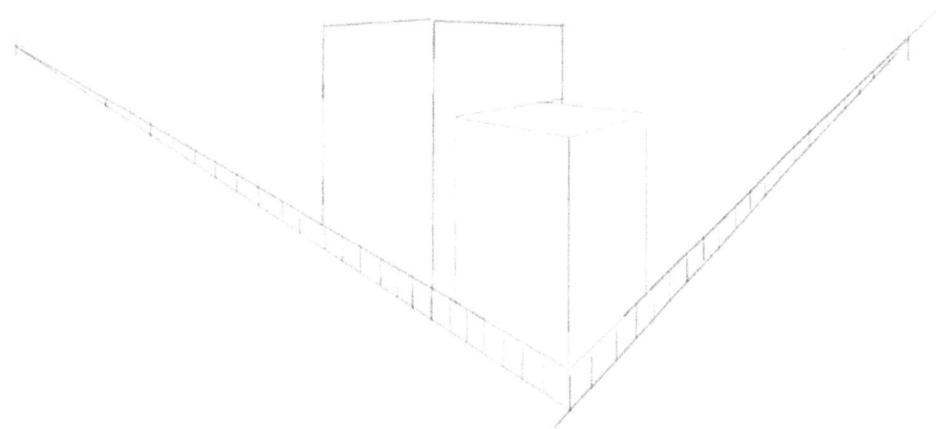

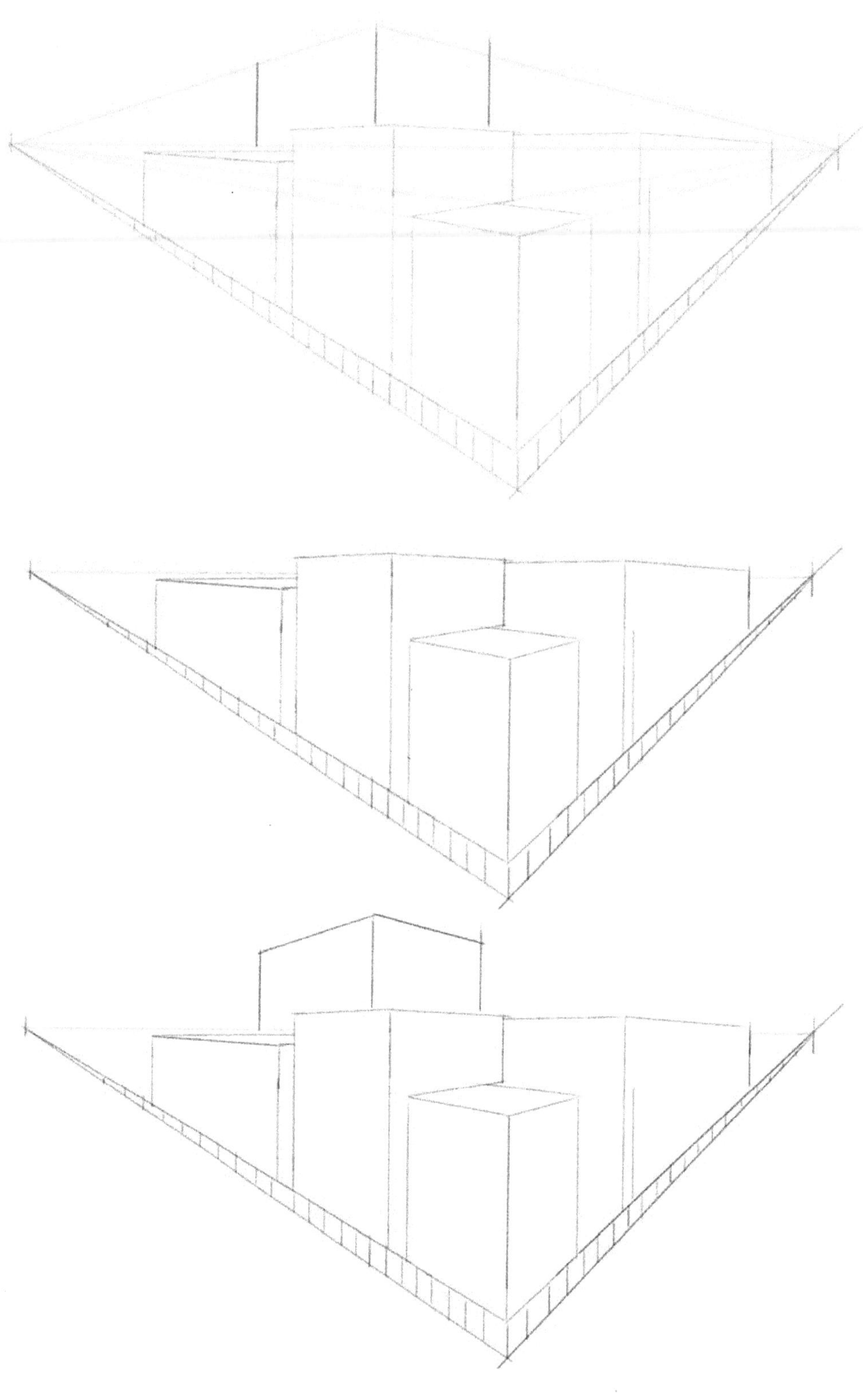

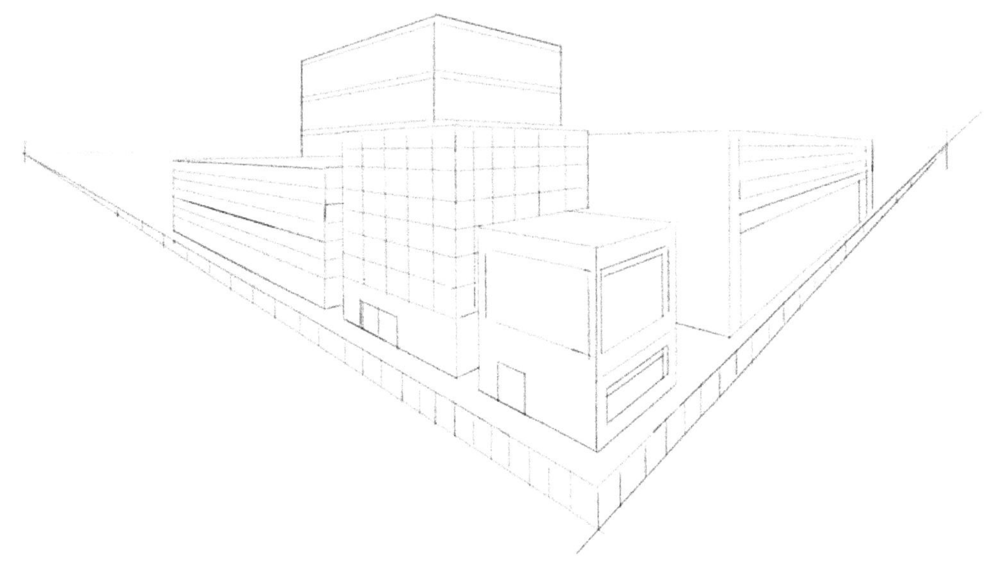

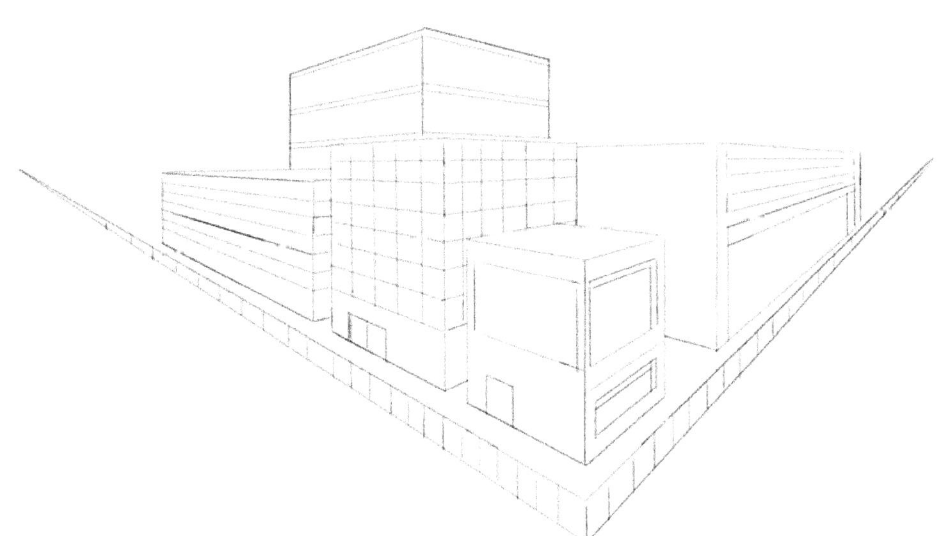

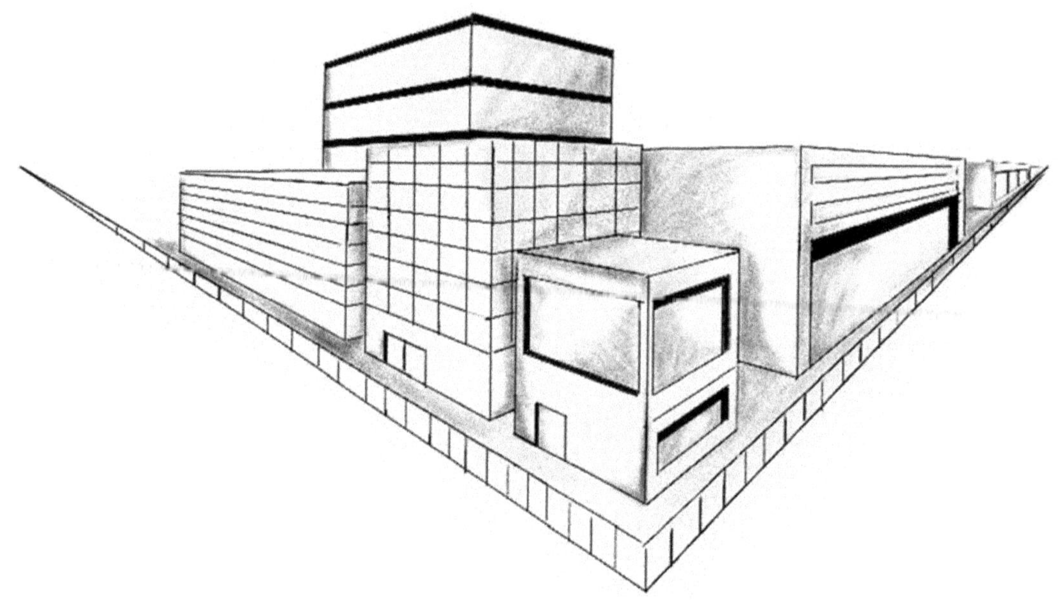

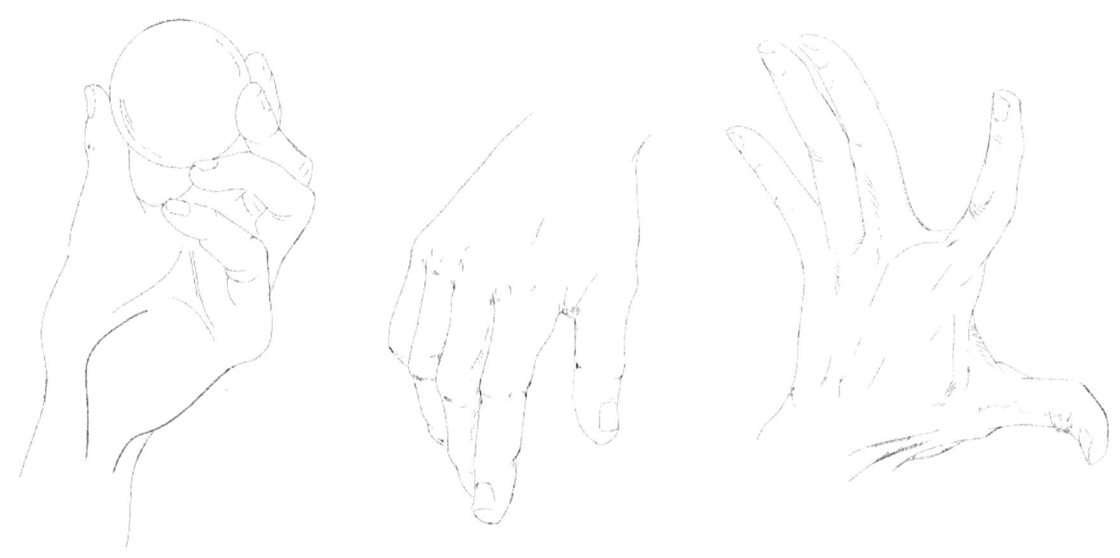

PART 3

MORE DRAWINGS

HANDS

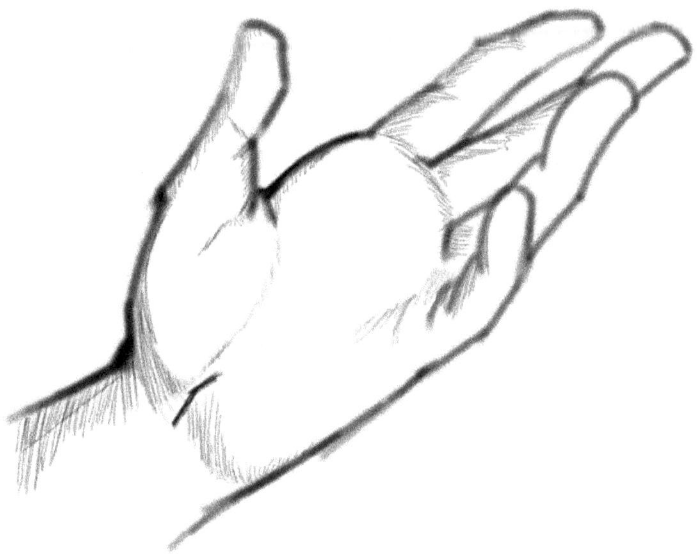

At some point in our artistic lives, we've all grappled with drawing hands. Hands can create beautiful drawings, but when I realized how many bones, muscles, and tendons there are to sketch, I just gave up for as long as I could.

Instead of hiding your characters' hands in their pockets or behind their backs, I'm going to walk you through the steps of drawing hands today.

The first step in drawing hands is to understand how to relate hands to your character's proportions and bone structure. We communicate a wide range of emotions with our hands using a variety of gestures, including sadness, fury, panic, and others.

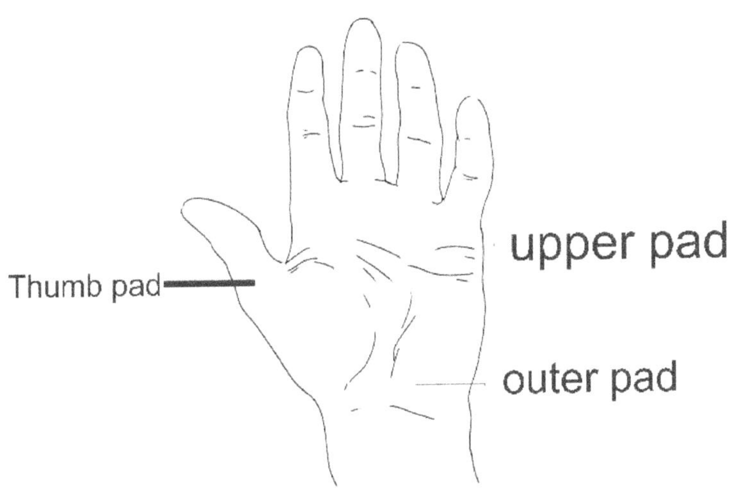
upper pad
Thumb pad
outer pad

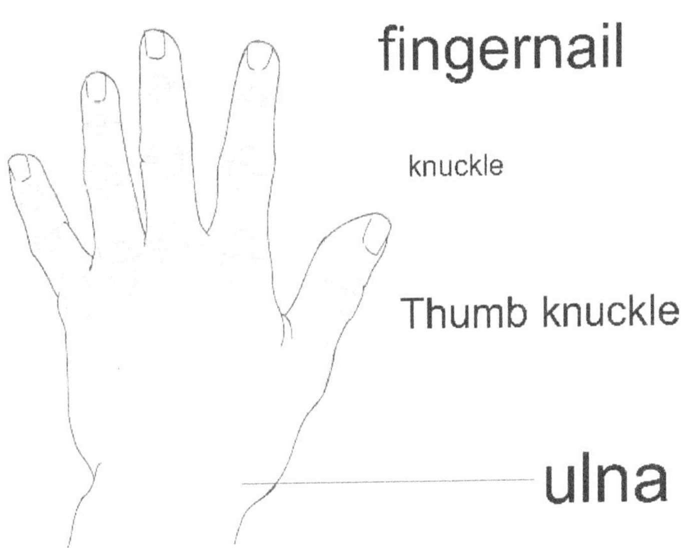
fingernail
knuckle
Thumb knuckle
ulna

DRAW A HAND

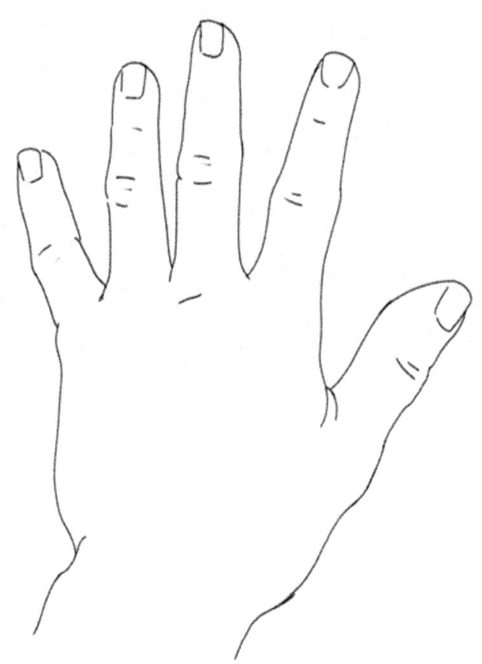

Make a rectangle the size of your hand.

With a line drawn across the rectangle, cut it in half.

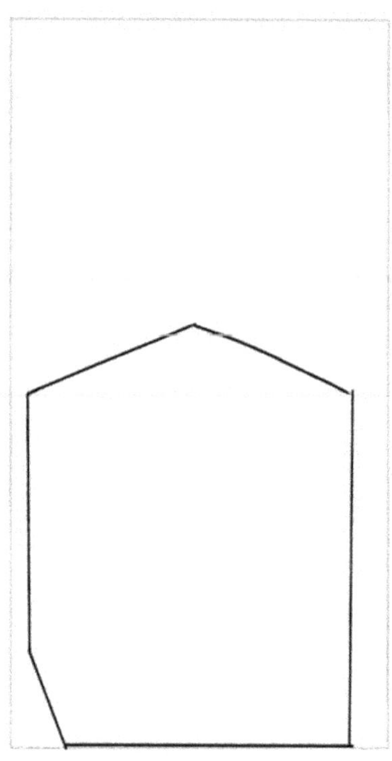

Make a drawing of your palm shape

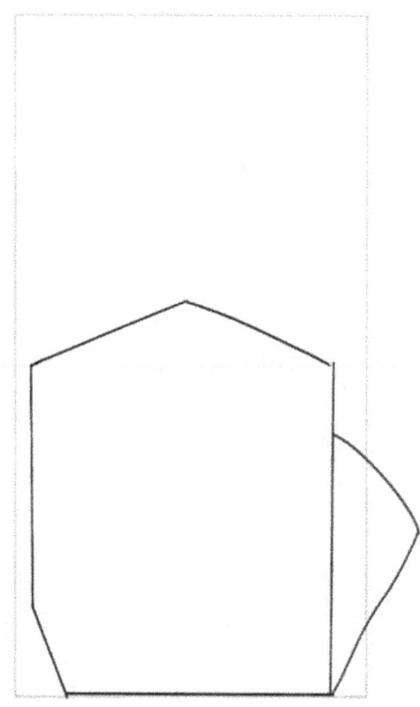

Make a little thumb shape Structure, check that it is as wide as your thumb when extended.

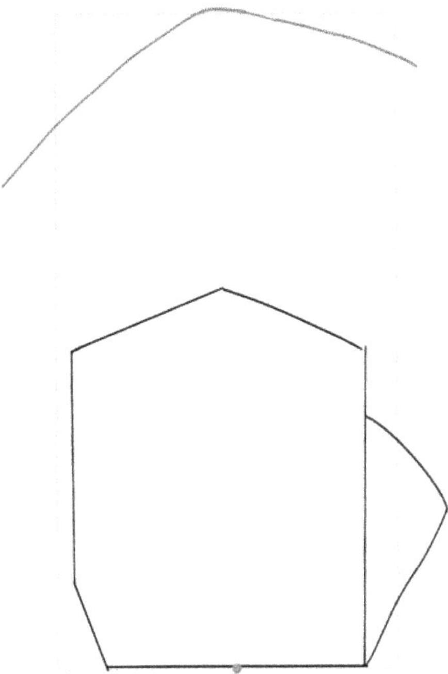

Draw a curving line across the top of the palm without crossing the square.

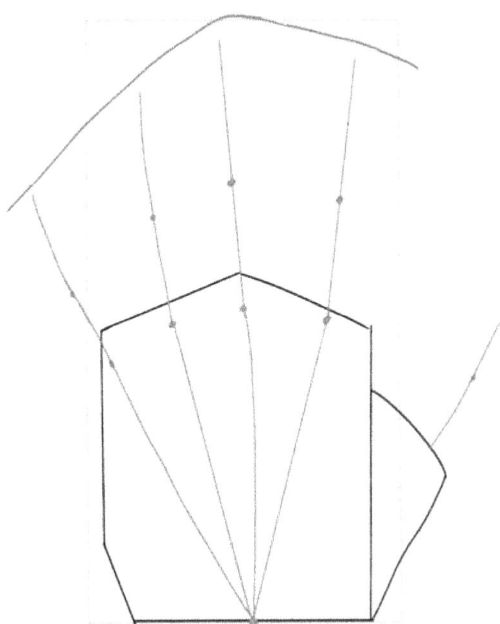

Draw the fingers, then the thumb and knuckles.

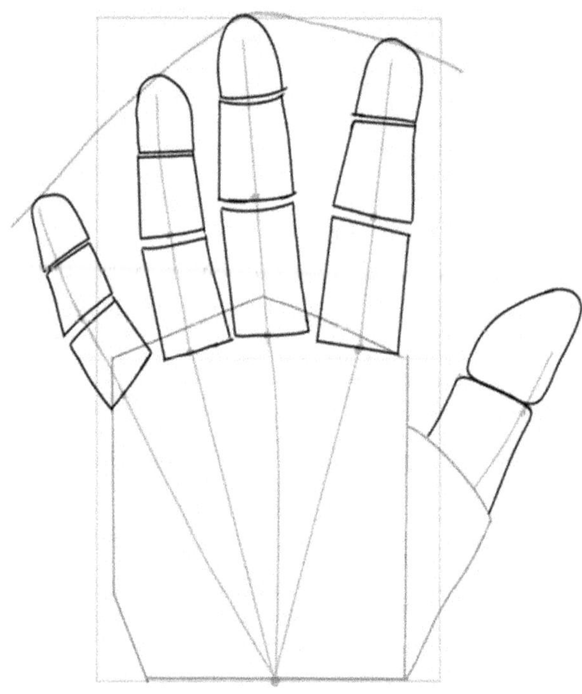

Remove your guidelines and begin working on the flesh. Using smooth and curved curves, draw the contour of your hand.

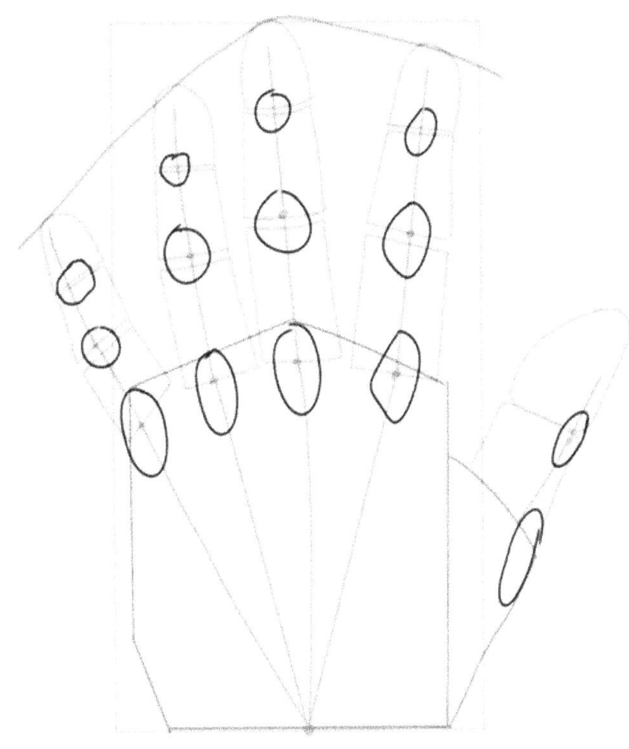

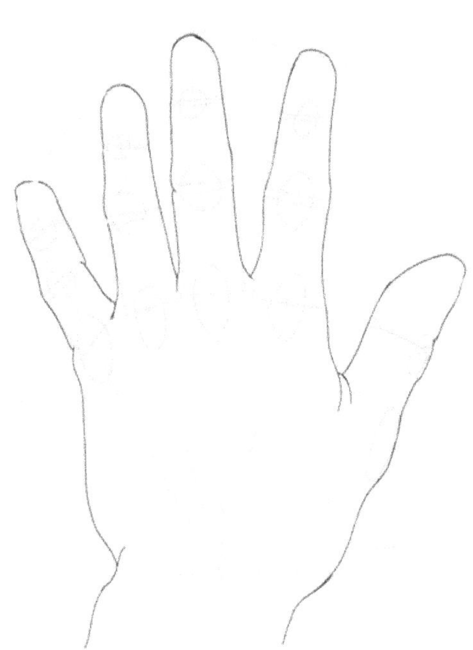

Include some flesh detail.

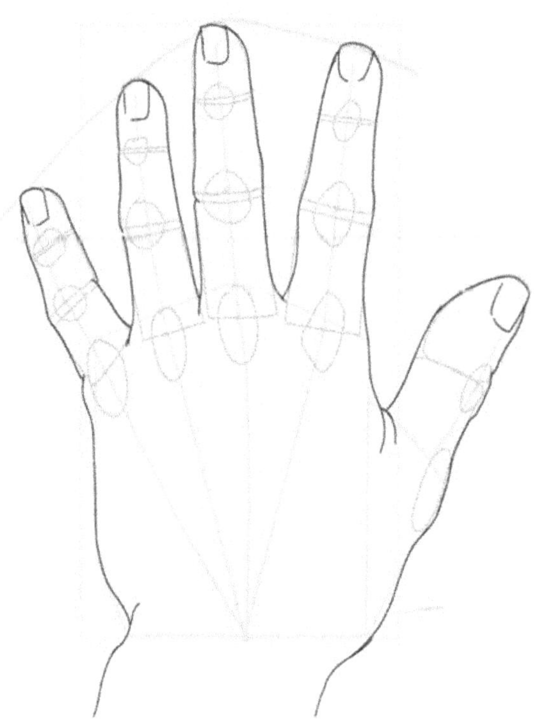

Add the nails now. Two curved lines going up and down and one curved line going across will do.

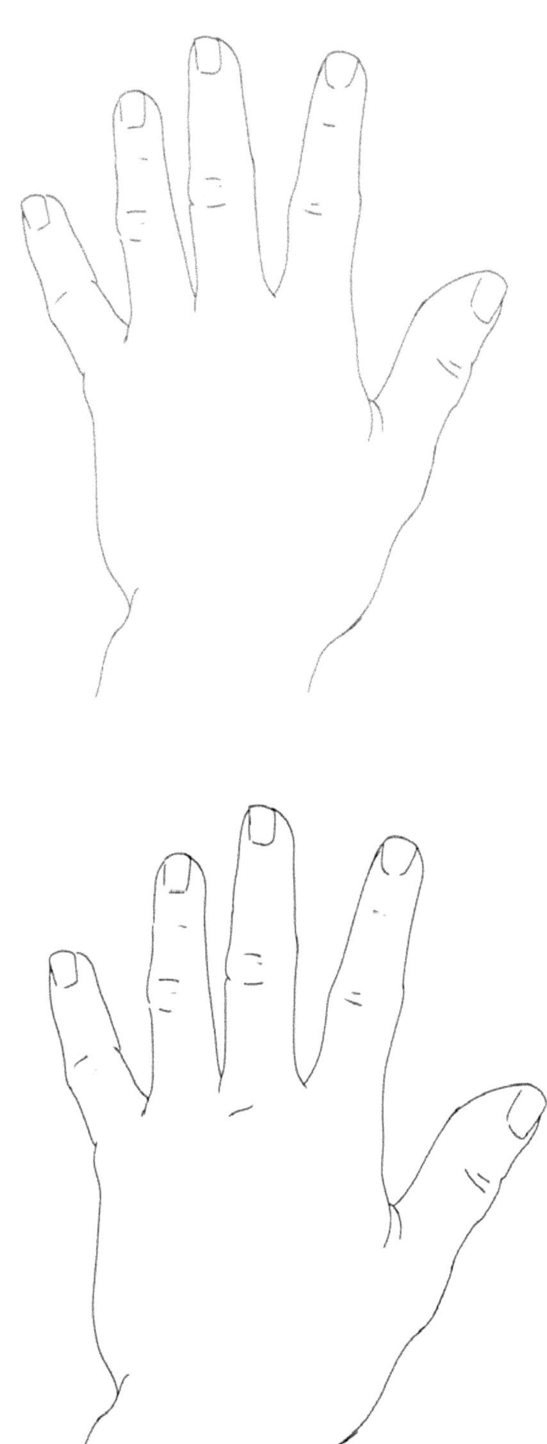

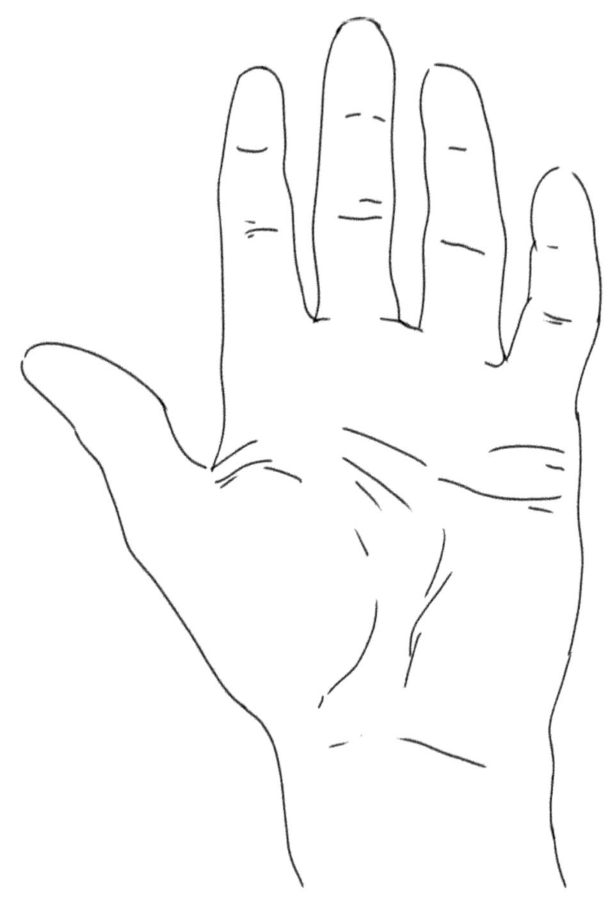

DRAW A PALM

Draw a square the size of your hand, then cut it in half.

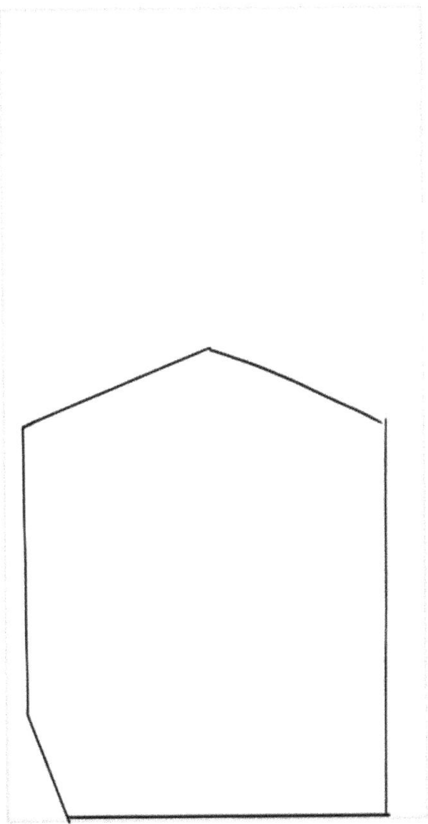

Draw the shape of the pal

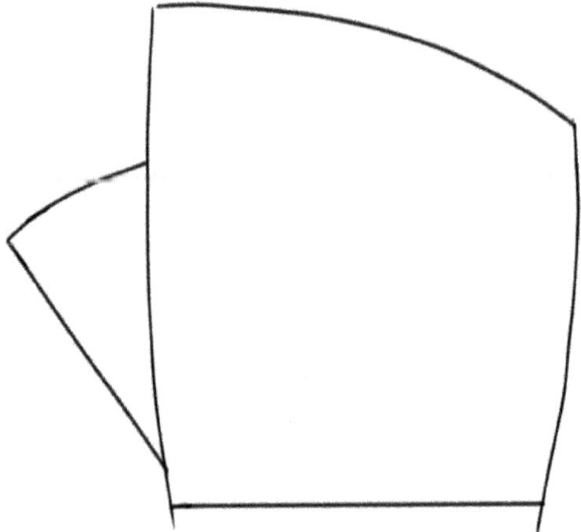

Add a small thumb form. Check the structure to make sure it's as wide as your thumb when it's stretched.

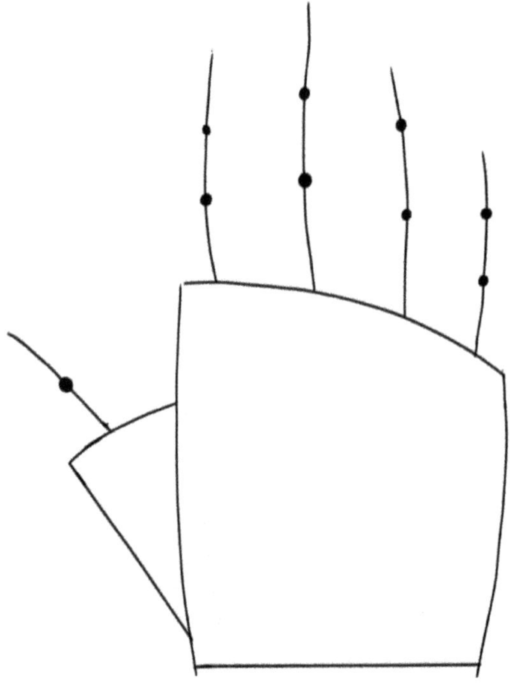

Create the Fingers

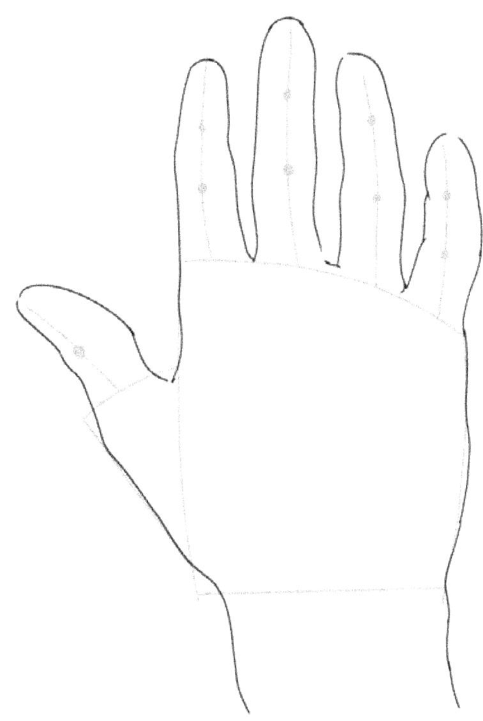

Build the flesh.

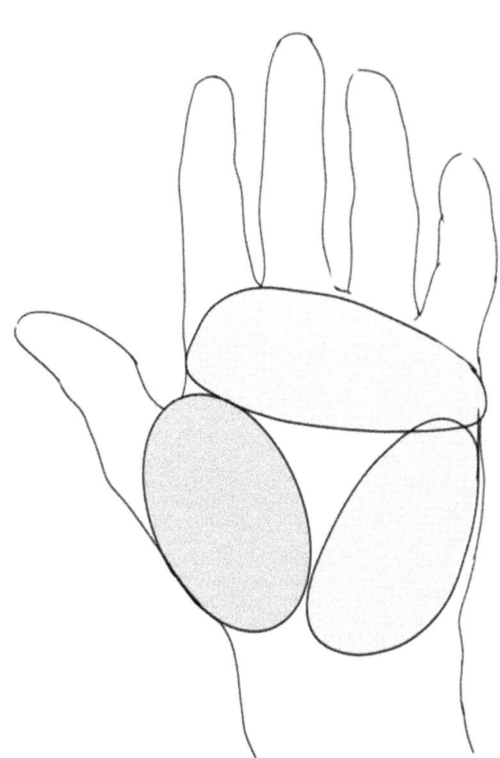

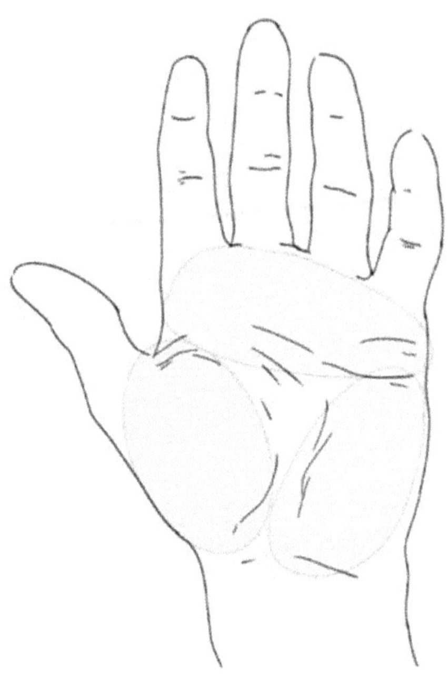

Small, curved lines should be used to draw your hand, taking into account the fingers and skin folds.

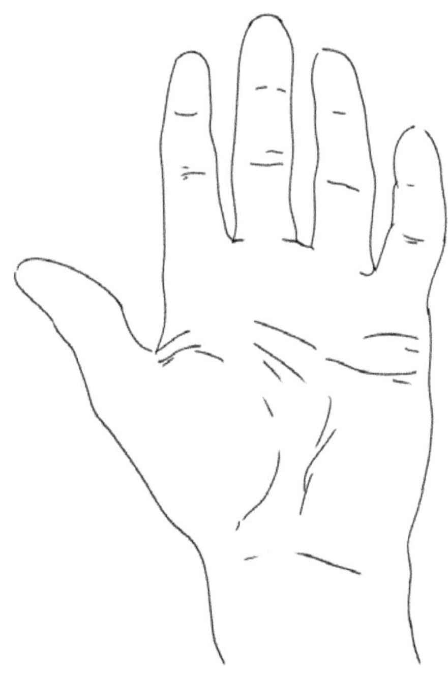

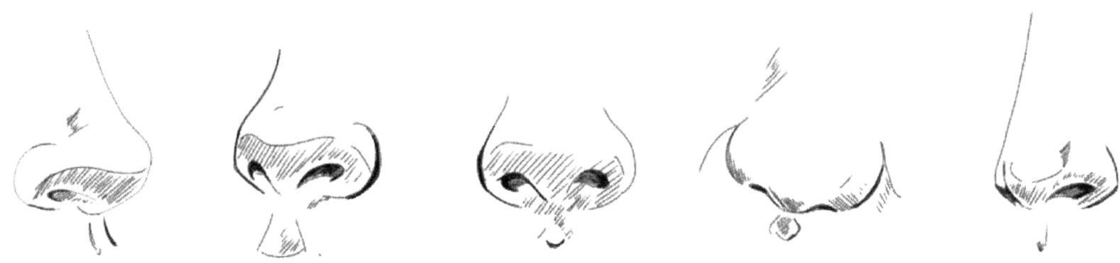

NOSE

DRAW A NOSE

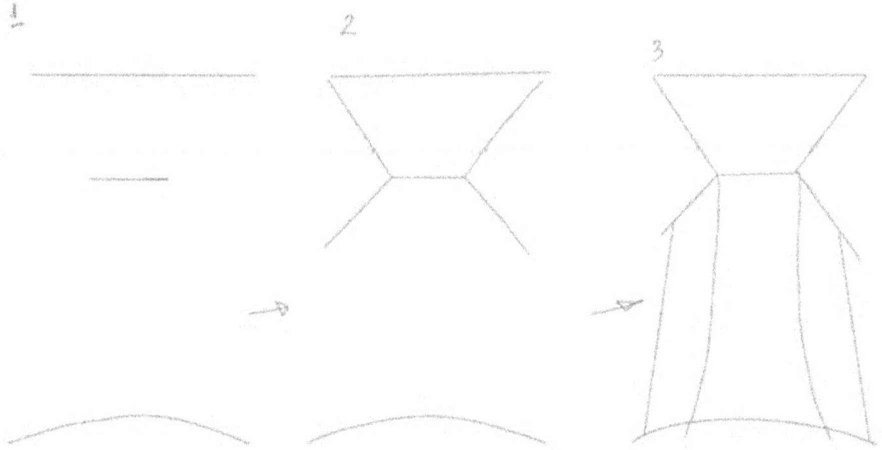

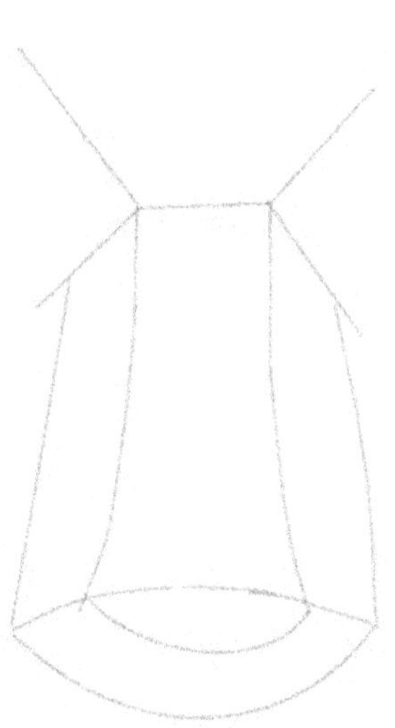

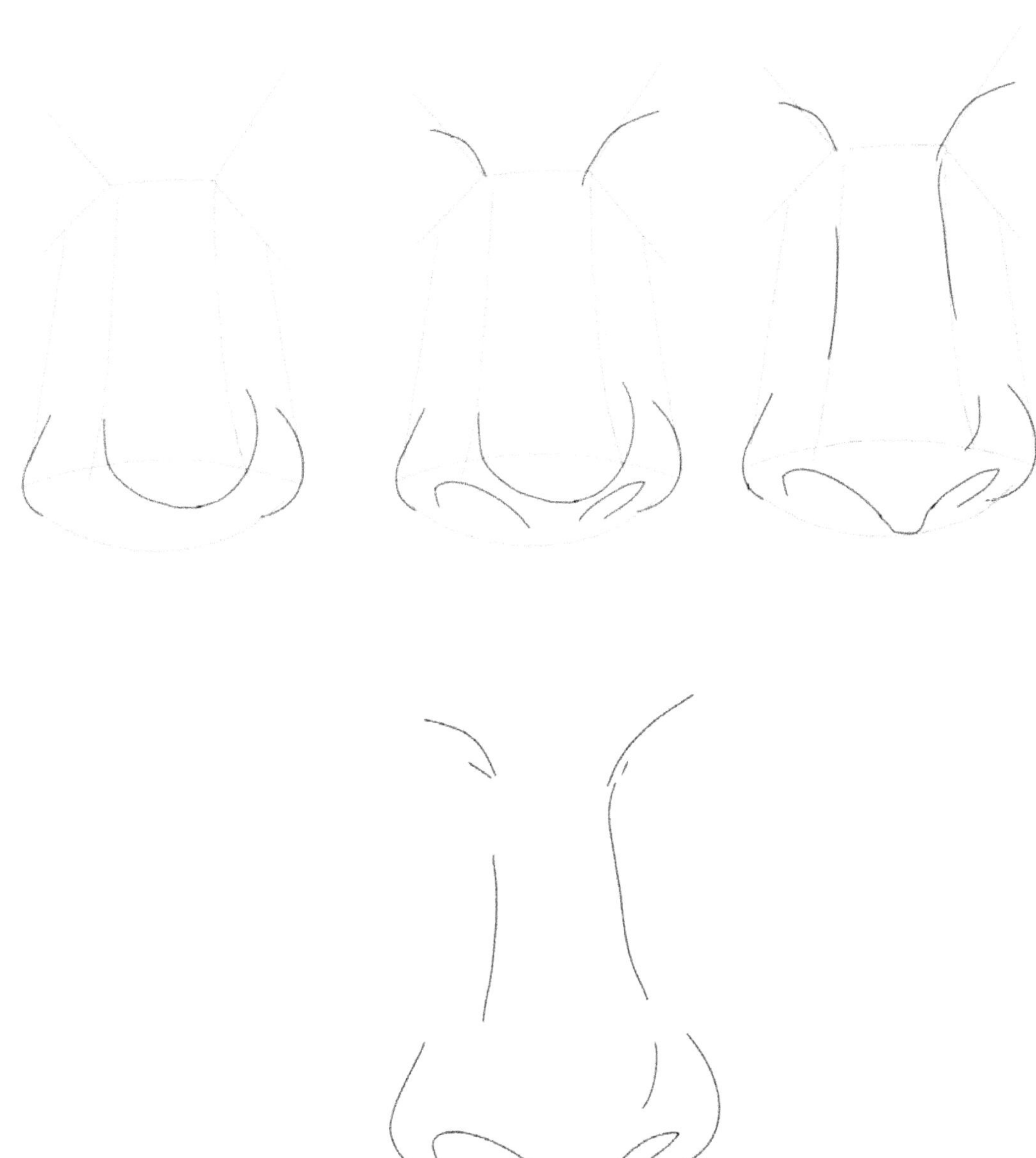

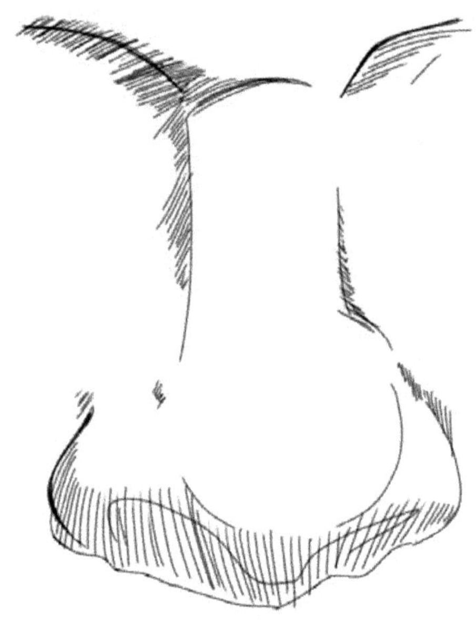

DRAW FROM THE SIDE VIEW

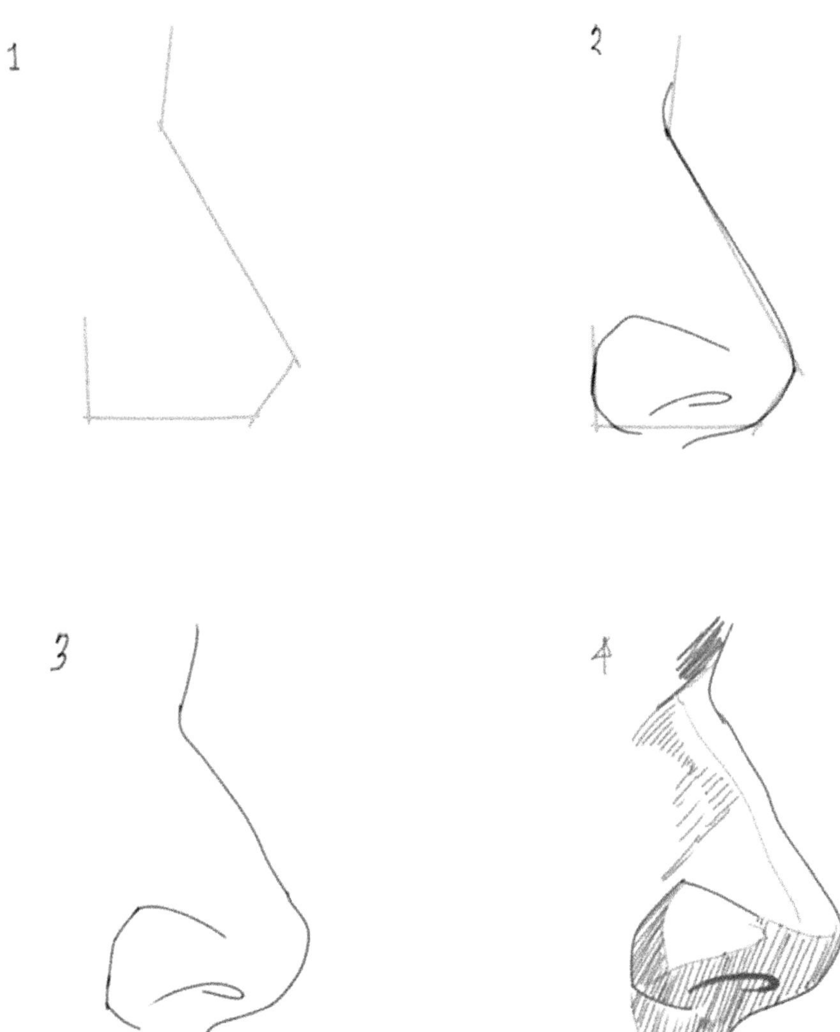

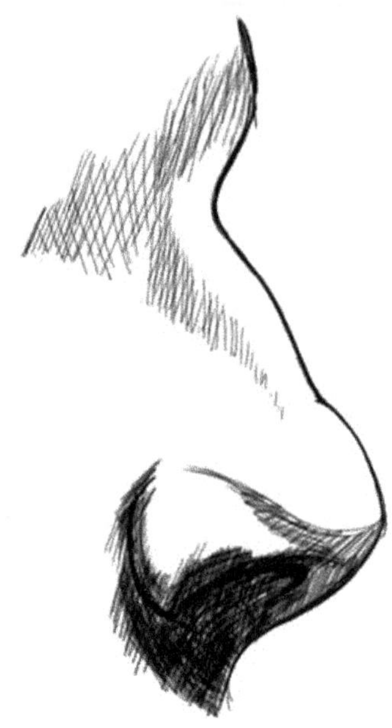

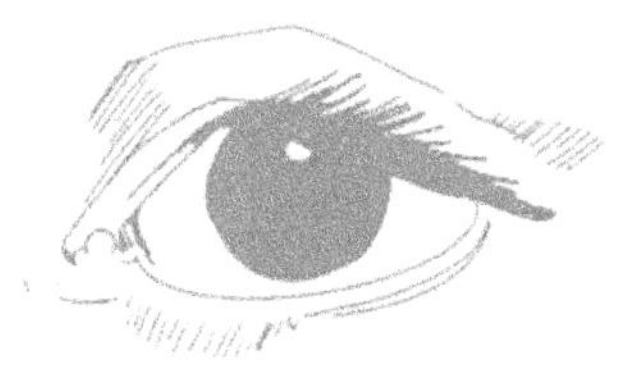 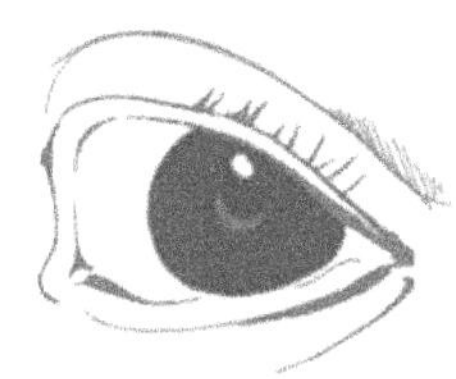 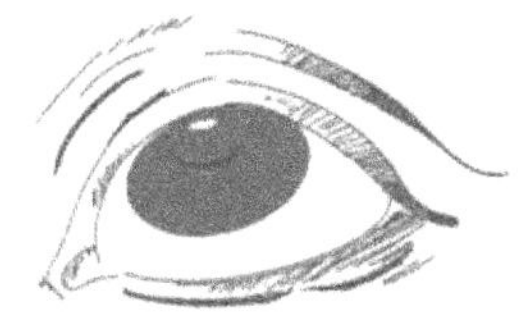

"the window to the soul". Sometimes we can look at just a person's eyes and know exactly who they are.

EYES

We'll look at how to draw an eye in this lesson. The process itself is pretty easy to understand.

Because each eye is different, you need to pay close attention to how the top and bottom eyelids are shaped. The better you can notice things, the more connections you will find.

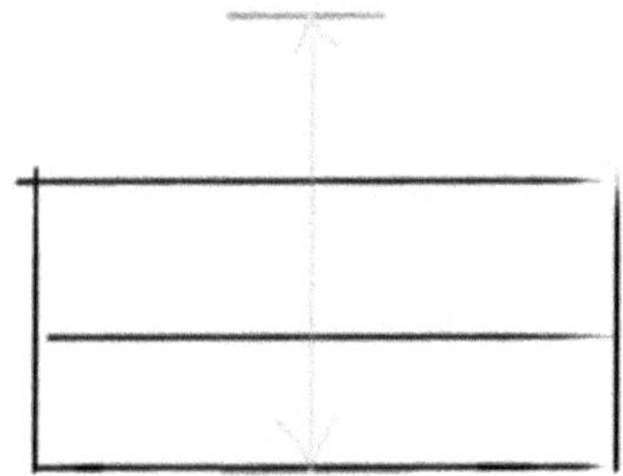

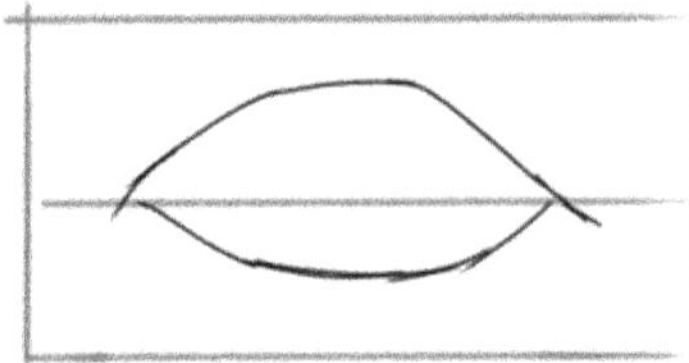

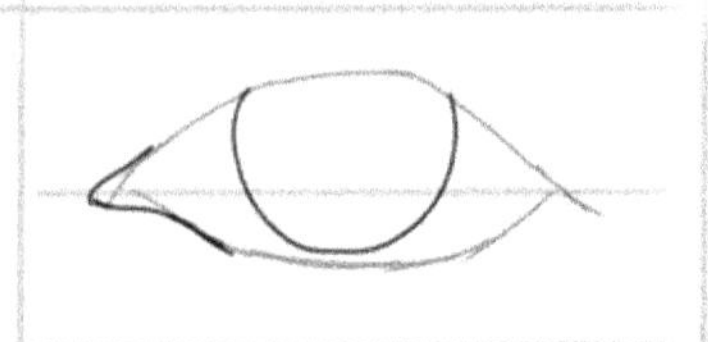

- Draw a small square, then cut it in half.

- Draw both eyes and then the cornea.

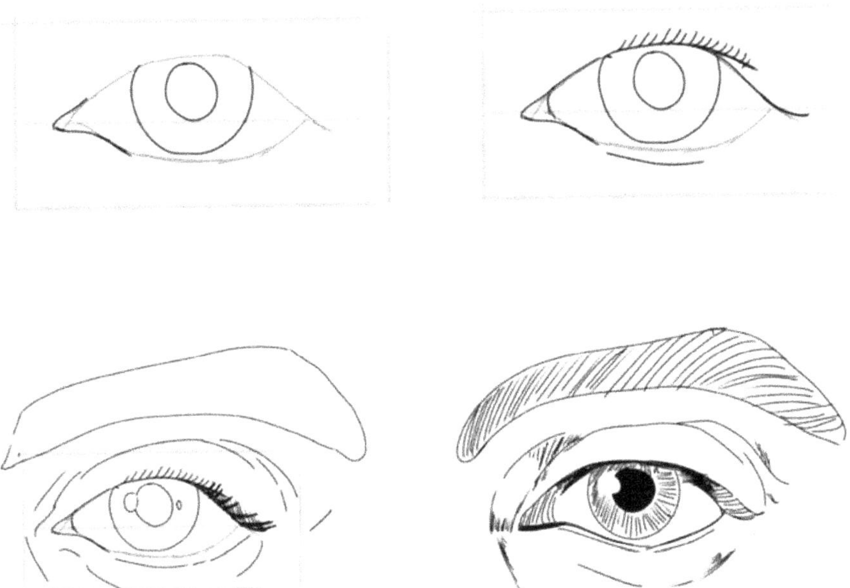

- Draw the cornea and add more details to the eyelid.
- Draw a few eyelashes and fill them in one at a time.
- Add the eyebrows and more details.

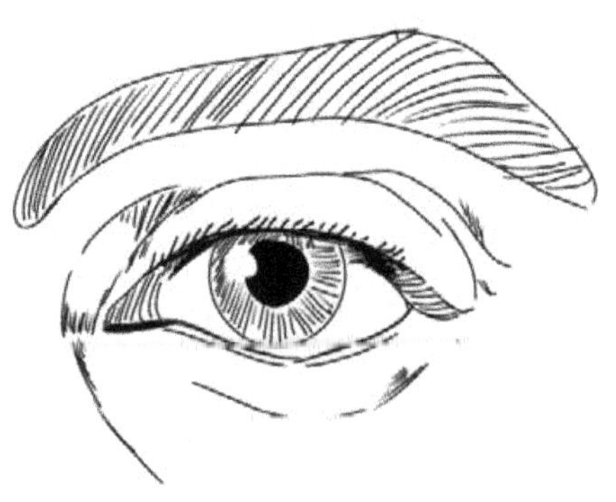

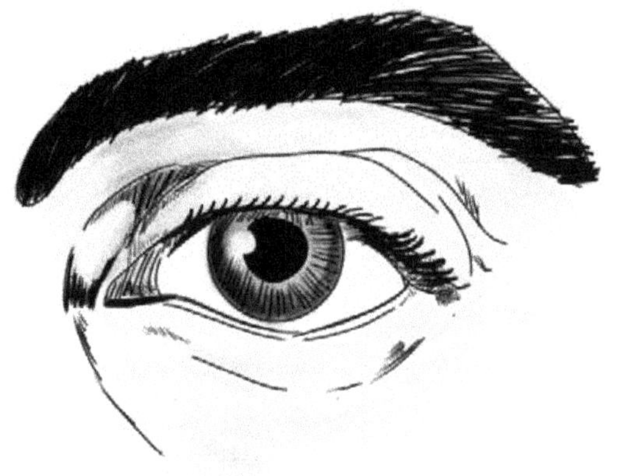

Utilize the hatching technique to add shading to your drawing.

DIFFERENT FROM THE SIDE VIEW

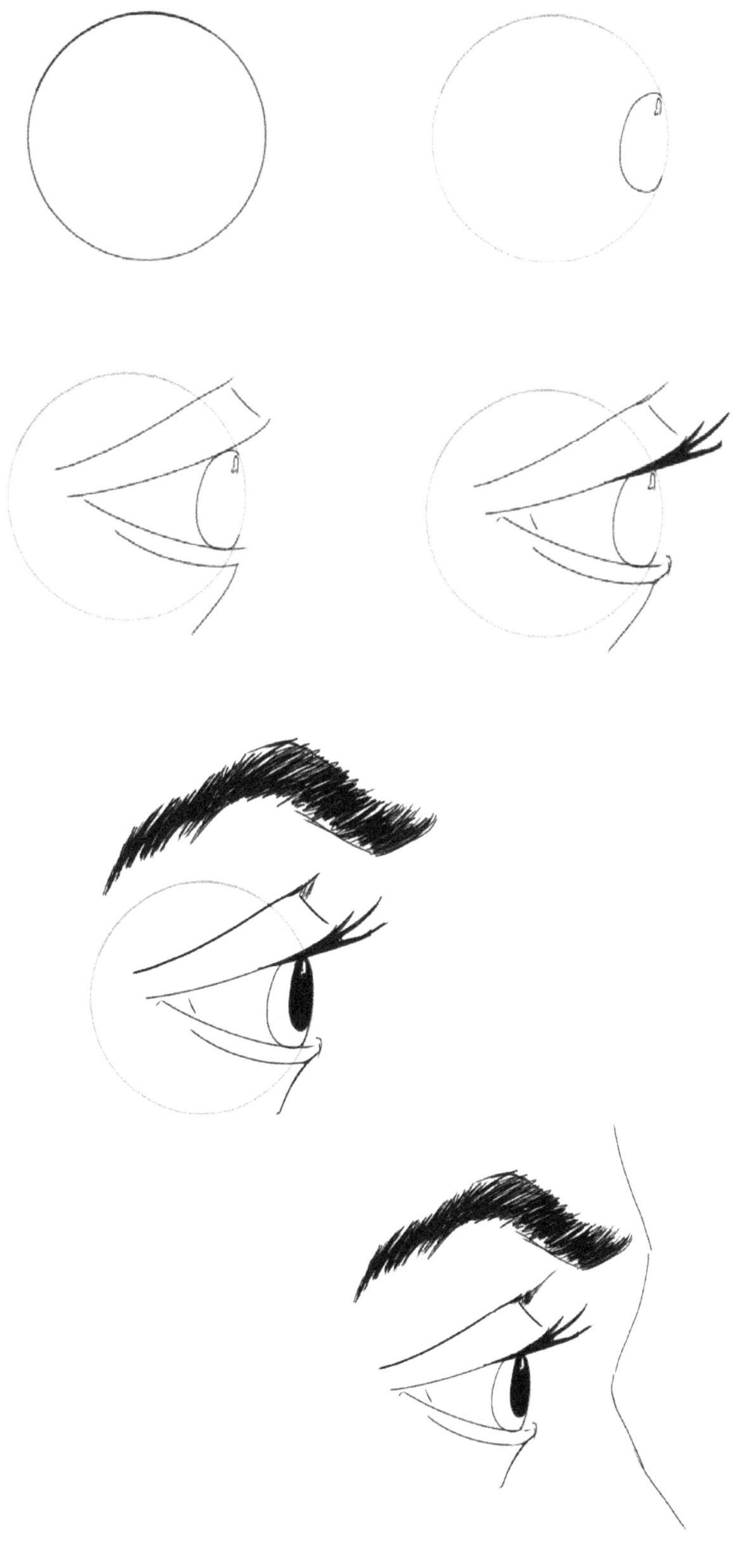

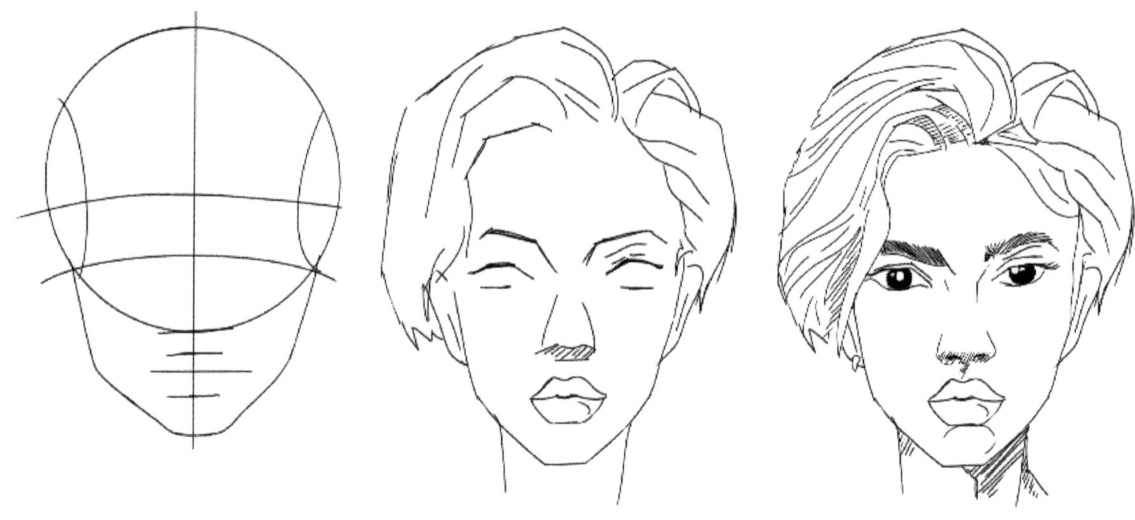

THE FACE

Drawing a Male Face

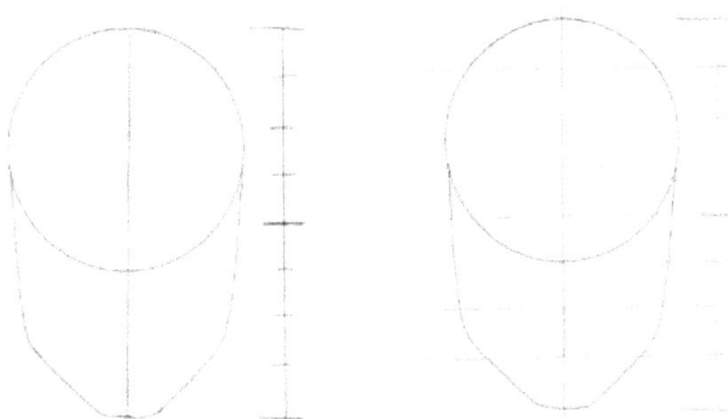

Start by drawing a big circle, then a straight line under it, and then the chin. Then, draw a straight line down the middle of the face to keep it balanced.

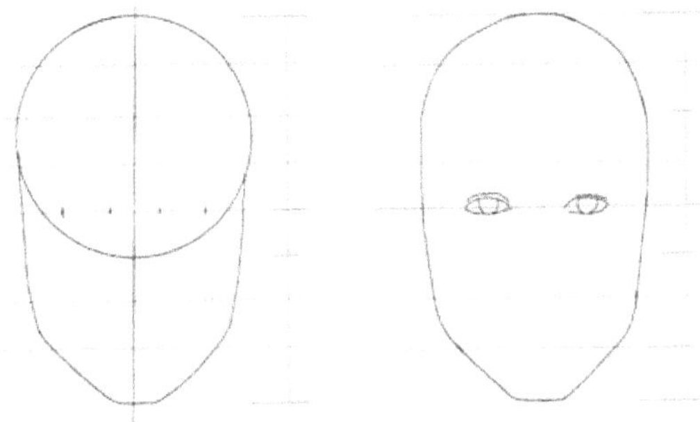

The hairline, eyebrows, eyes, nose, and mouth are all good places to use four or five horizontal lines to divide your drawing into parts. After that, add the eye and then the nose. The two lines don't have to be straight as long as they meet at the nose.

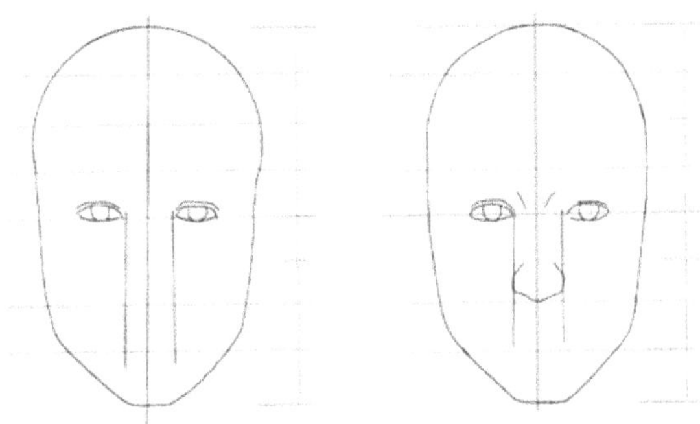

Start drawing the nose, making sure that the bridge of the nose stays inside the line. You should also add the eye hair. Remember that a man's brow needs to be thicker, while a woman's usually needs less hair.

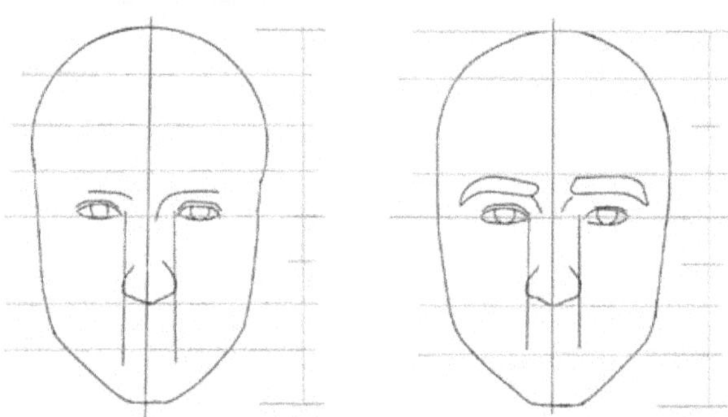

Draw a new vertical line from the middle of each eye down to the mouth. This will show where the upper lip meets the mouth.

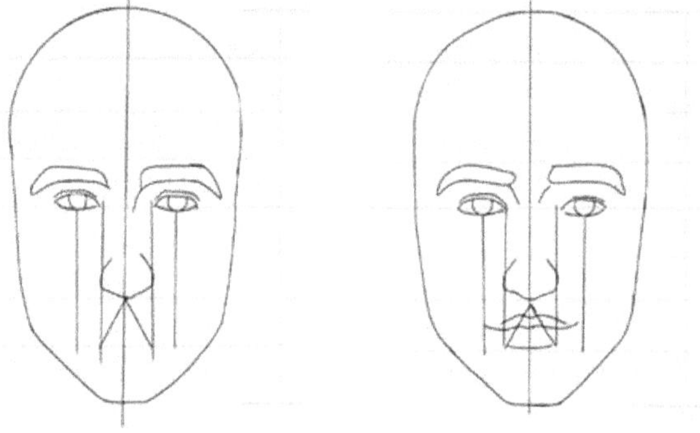

For the mouth, draw a triangle that begins from the center of the nose, this would help in drawing the lips

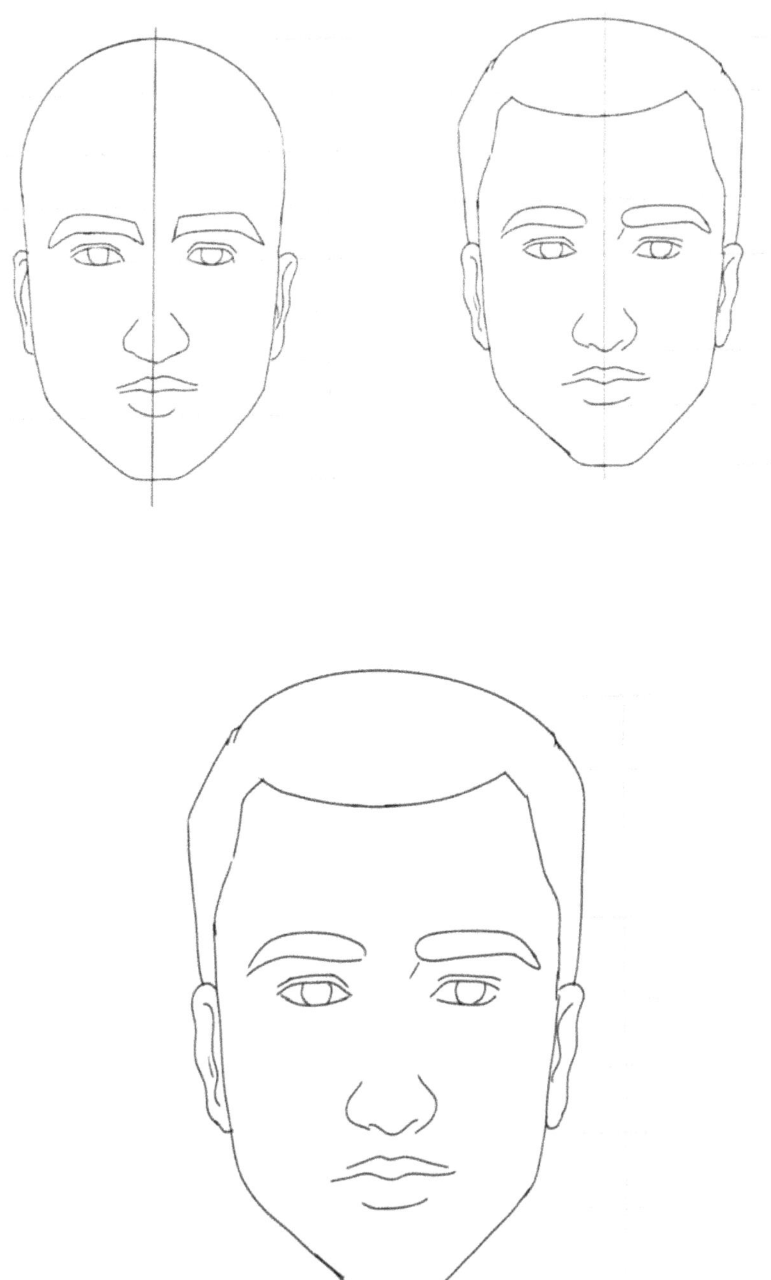

Draw the ears and the top edge of the hair. Start giving the drawing more features by coloring in the eyebrows and then the eyes. Start shading with your pencil, making sure to make some spots darker to show value and depth.

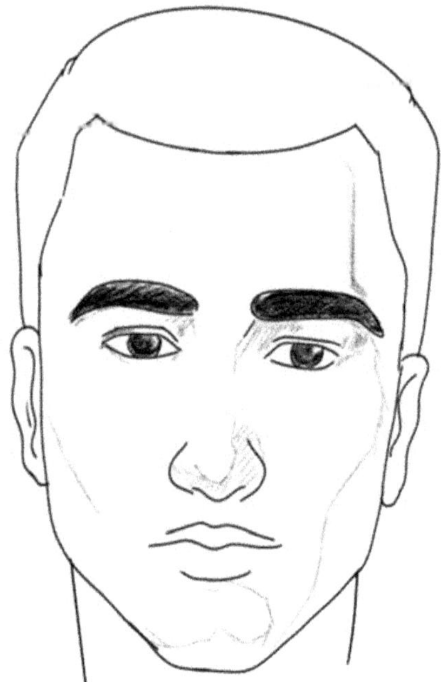

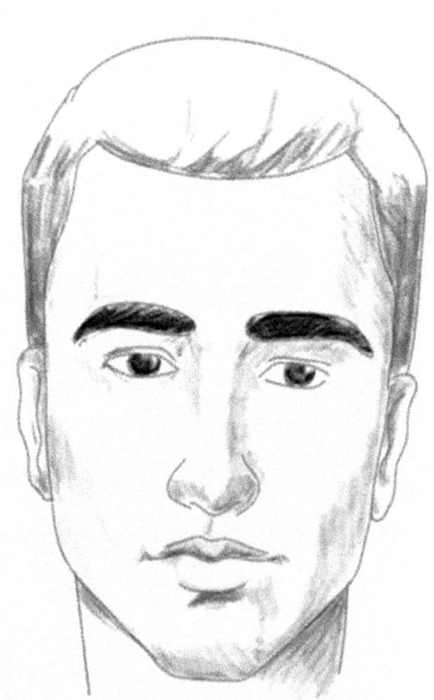

Viola!

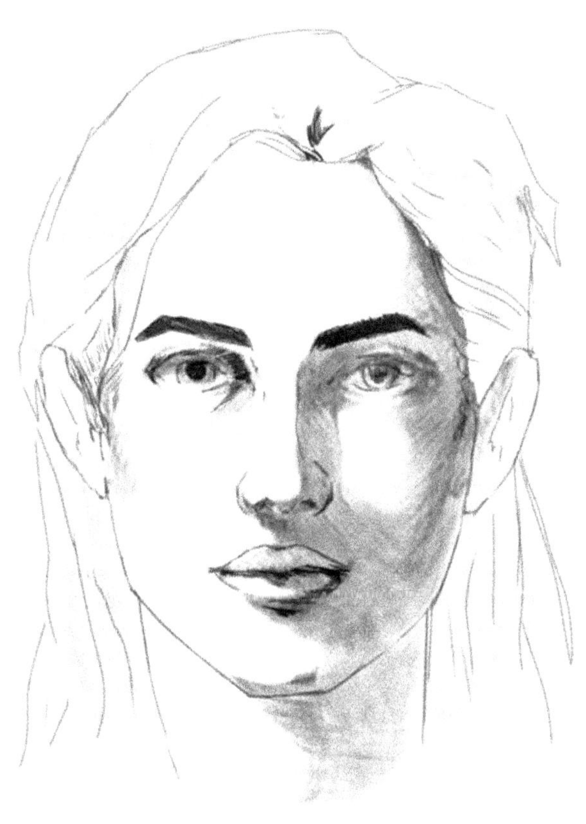

DRAWING A FEMALE FACE

To start, create a huge circle, a horizontal line beneath it, and then draw the jawline. After that, draw a vertical line in the center of the face to keep the symmetry of the face.

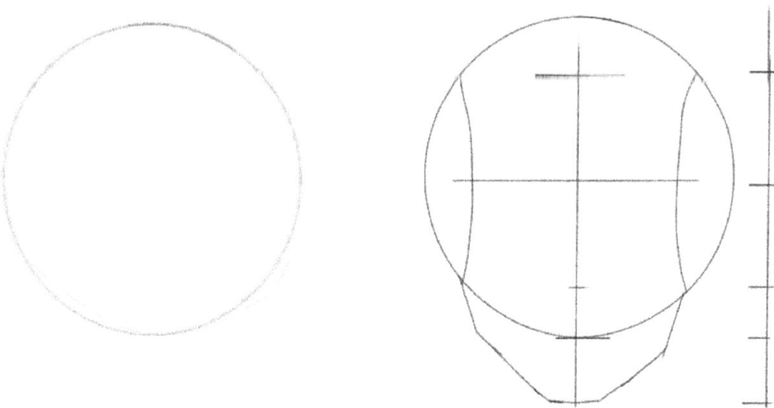

Divide your drawing into sections with four to five horizontal lines spaced widely apart at important points like the hairline, brows, eyes, nose, and mouth. Next, add the iris, and finally the nose. The two lines don't have to be straight as long as they extend downward to the level of the nose.

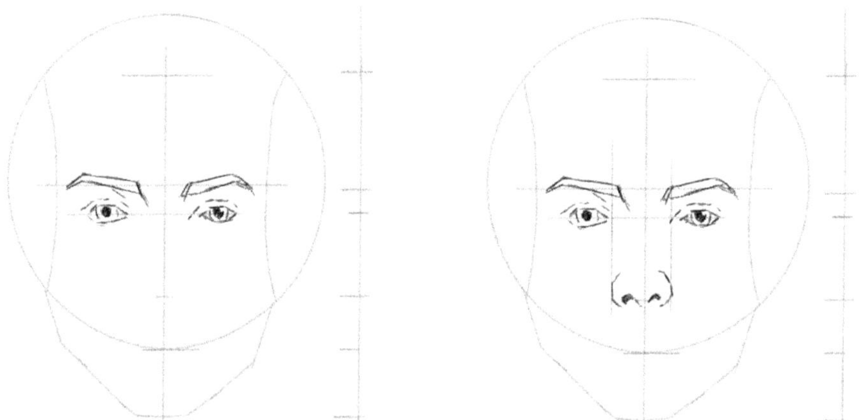

Begin Drawing the nose, being careful to keep the boundaries of the bridge of the nostril within the line. The eye brow should also be added. Remember, if you are drawing a woman, she needs to have less hair.

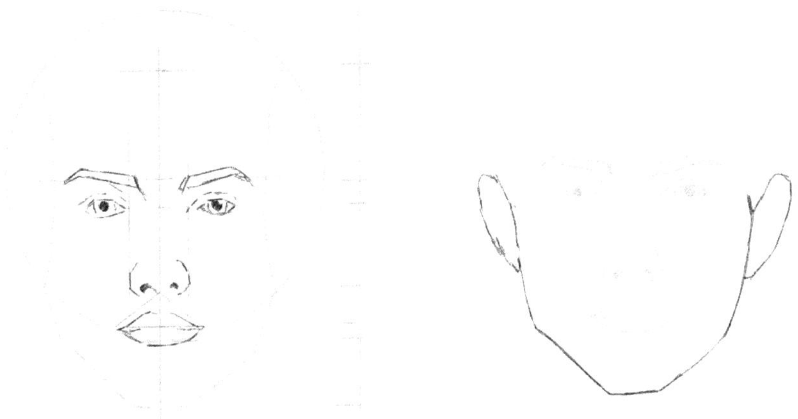

Draw a new, vertical line from the middle of each eye down to the mouth; this will show where the outer lip and mouth meet. For the mouth, draw a triangle that begins from the center of the nose, this would help in drawing the lips

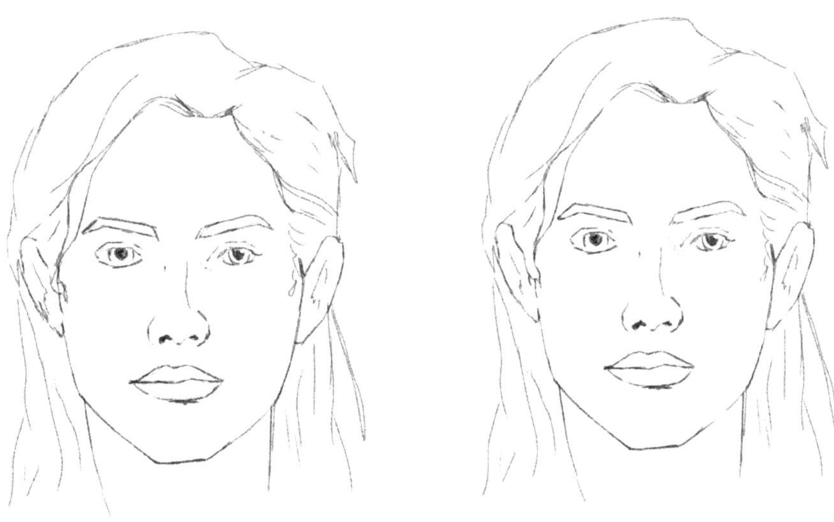

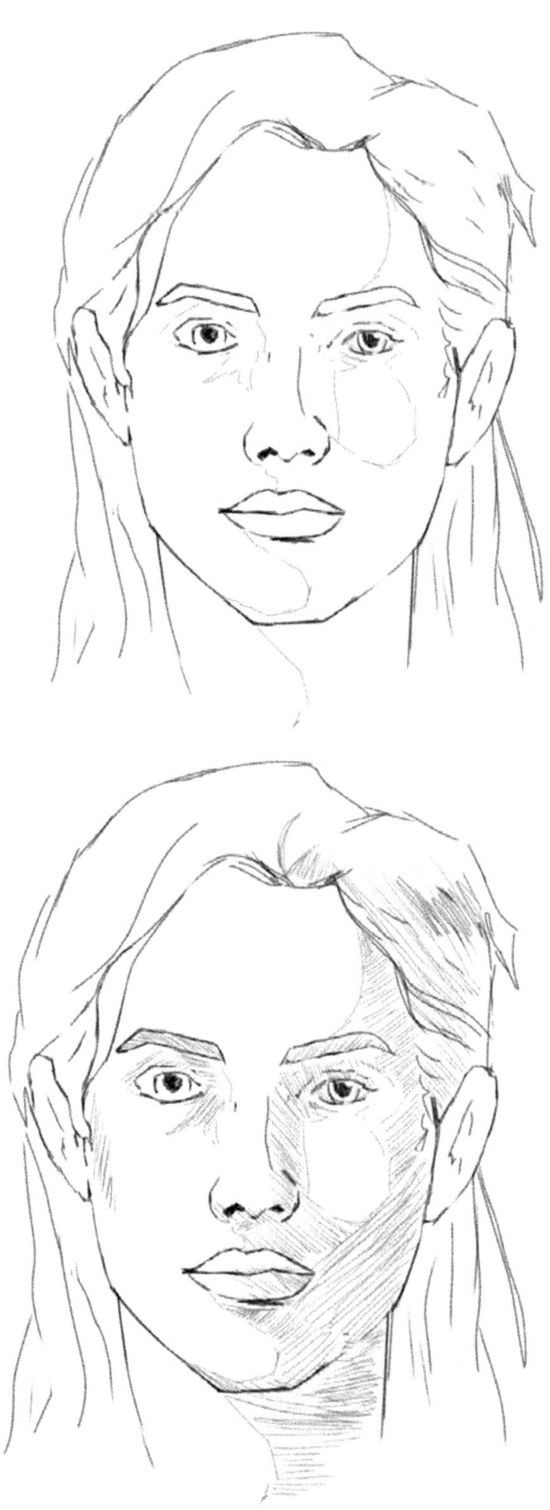

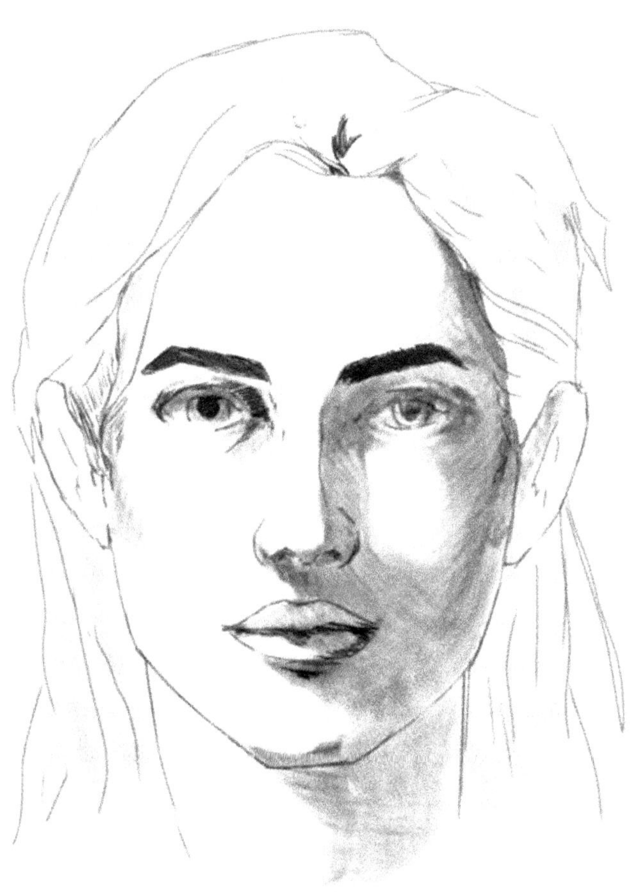

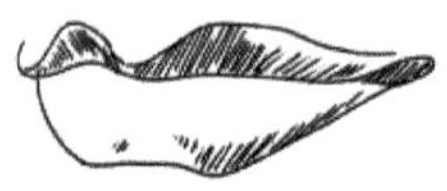
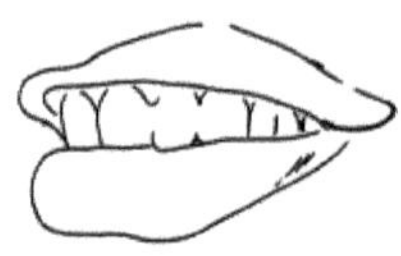
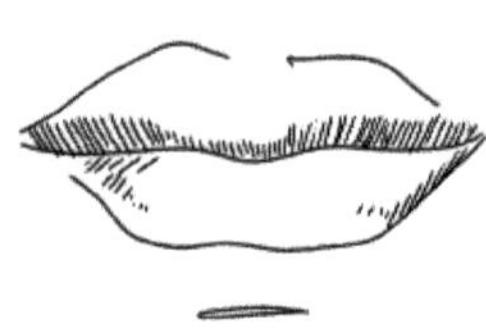
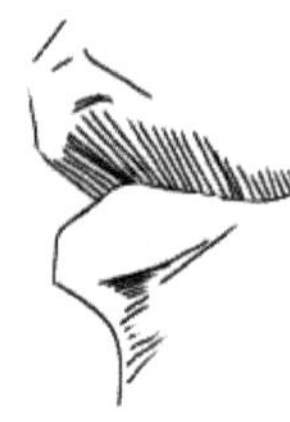

MOUTH

The Lips

The upper lip is divided into the middle portion and two edges that slope downward, whereas the lower lip is separated into the lower and upper lips.

For reference, here are some pictures of lips:

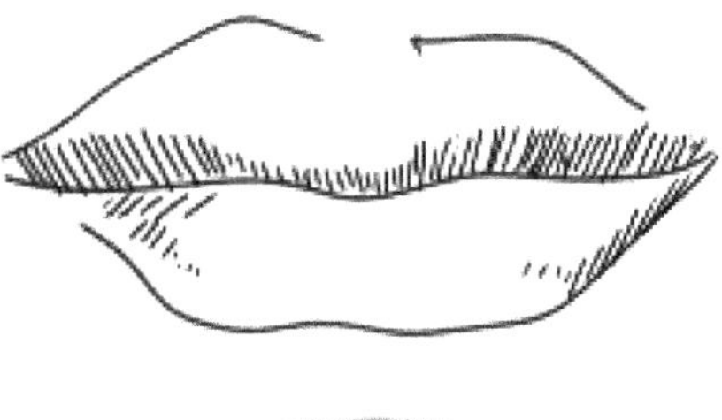

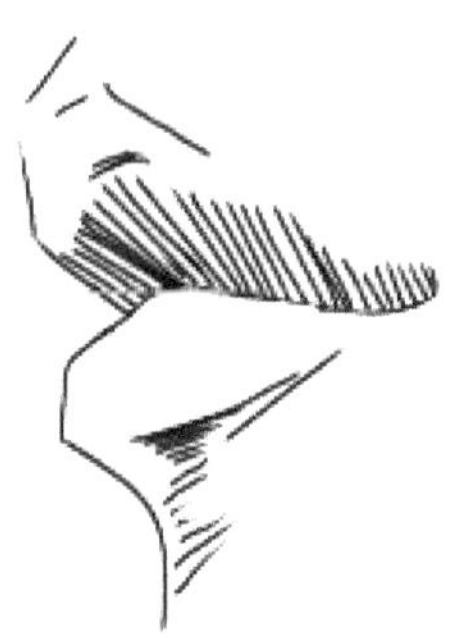

FULL LIPS

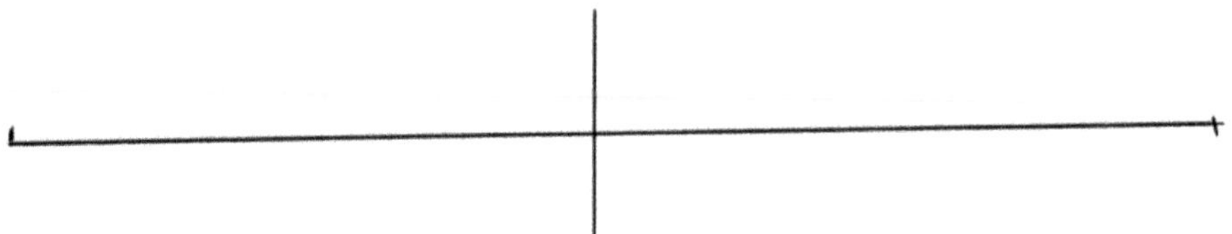

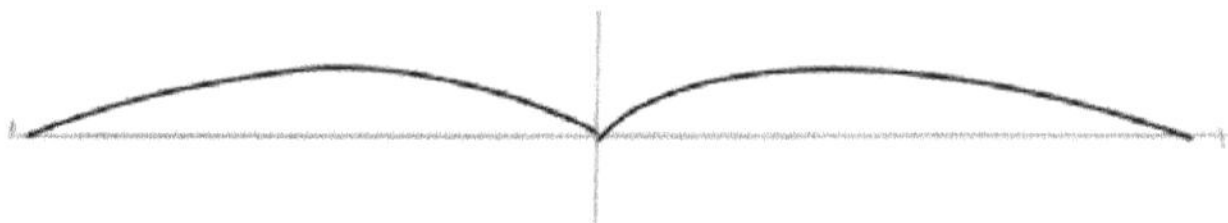

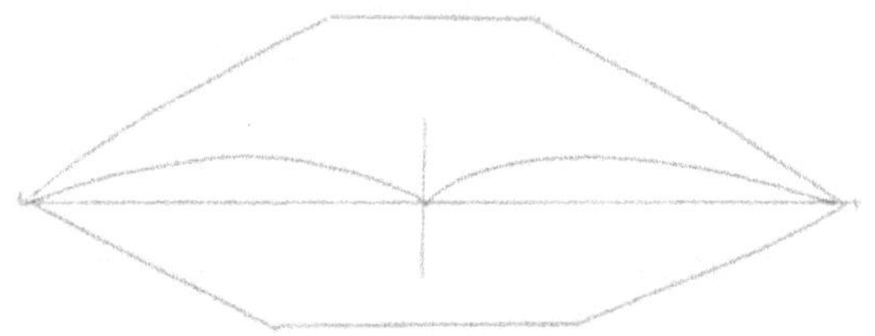

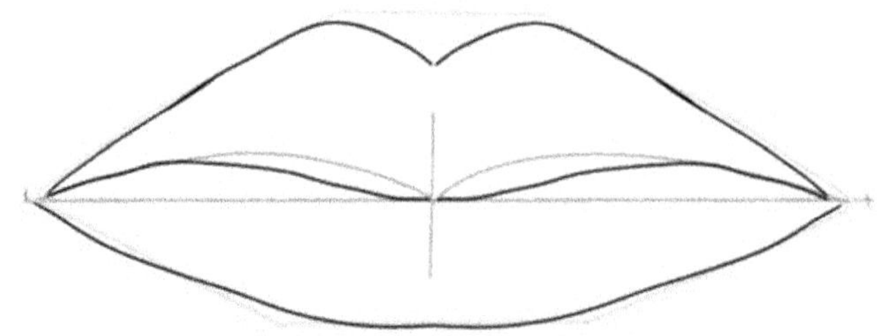

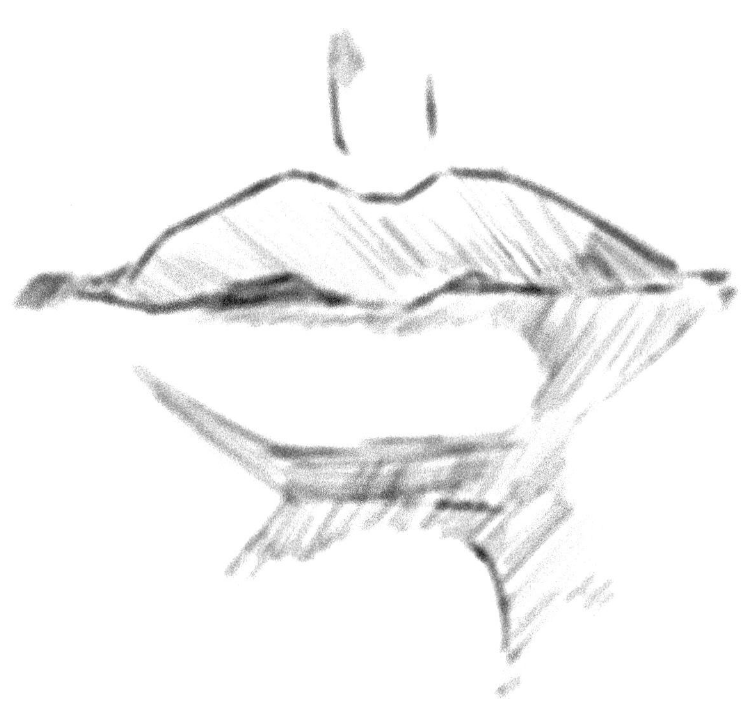

SIDE LIPS

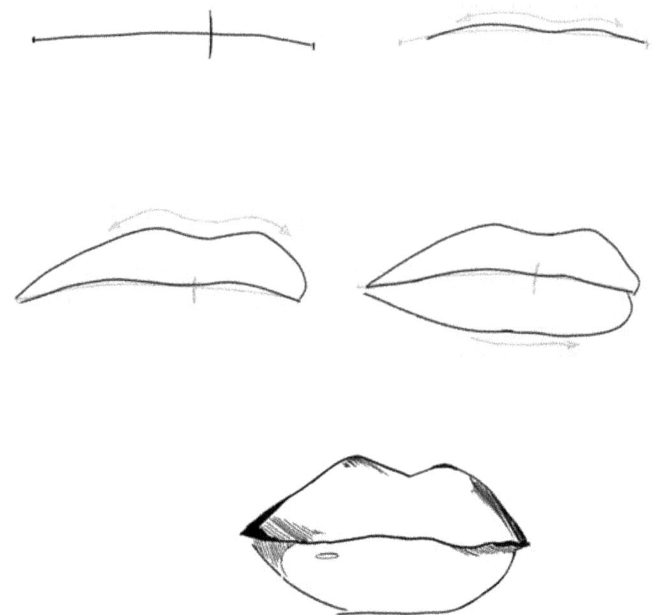

SIDE PROFILE

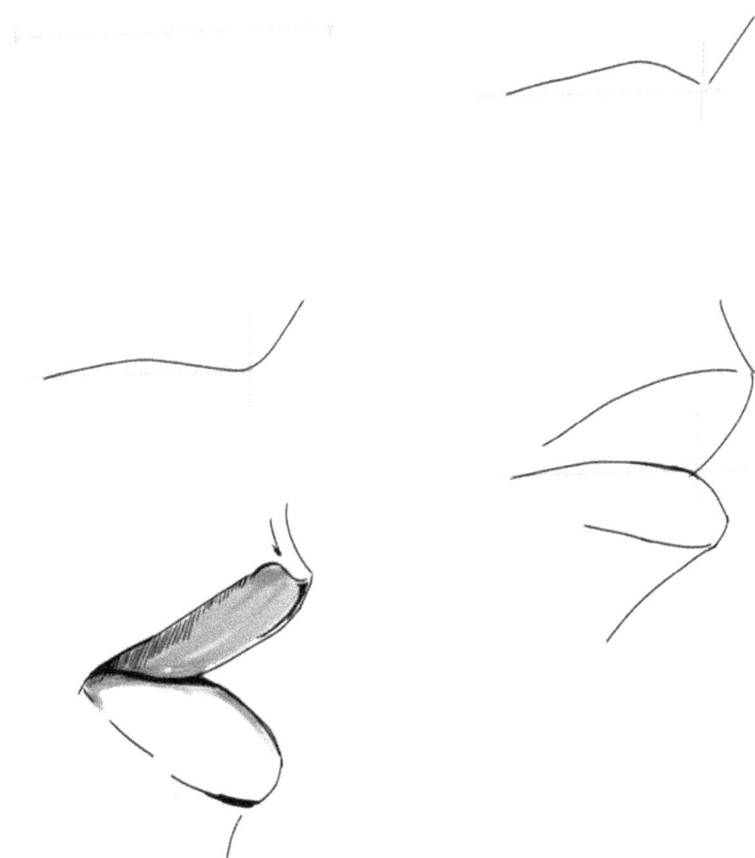

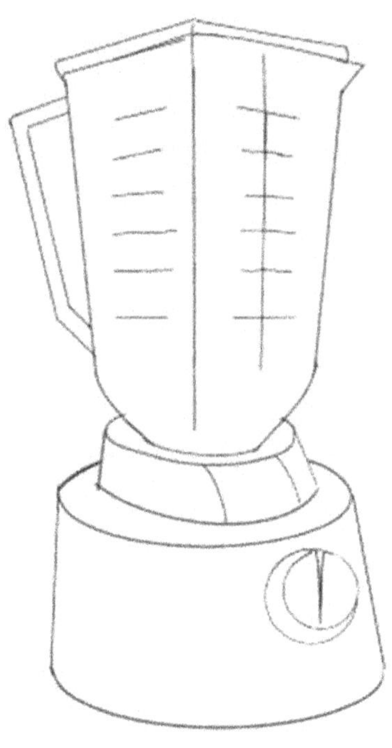

BLENDER

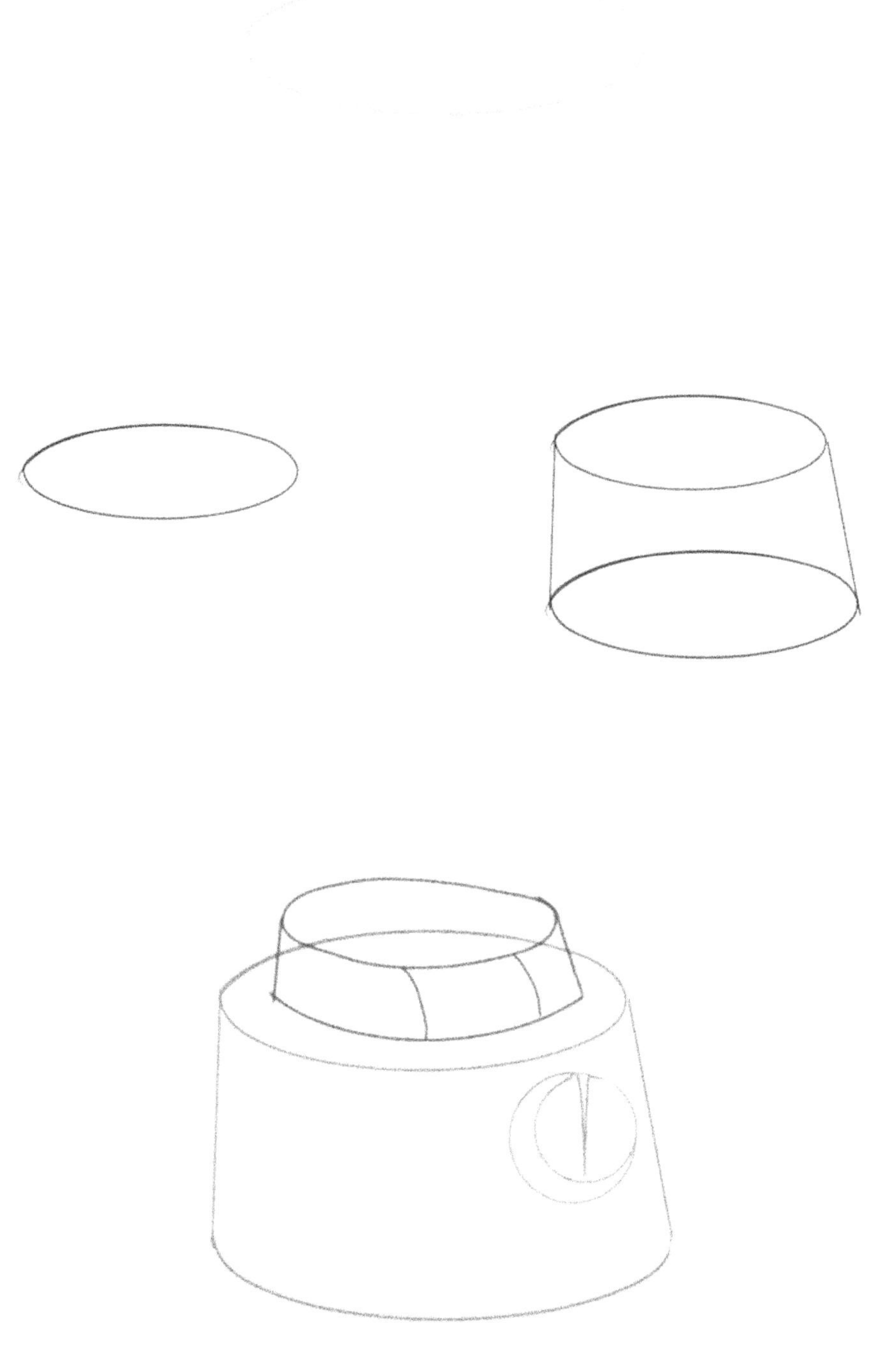

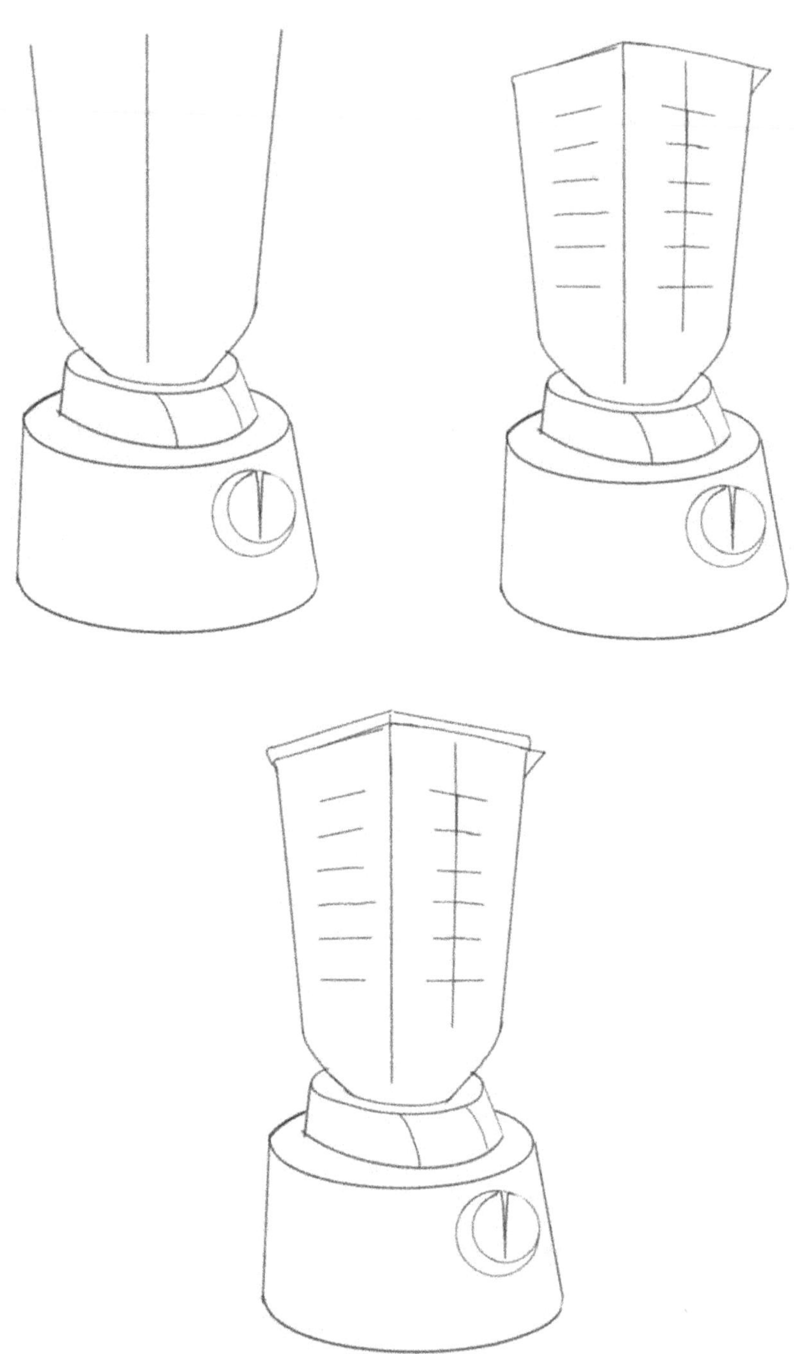

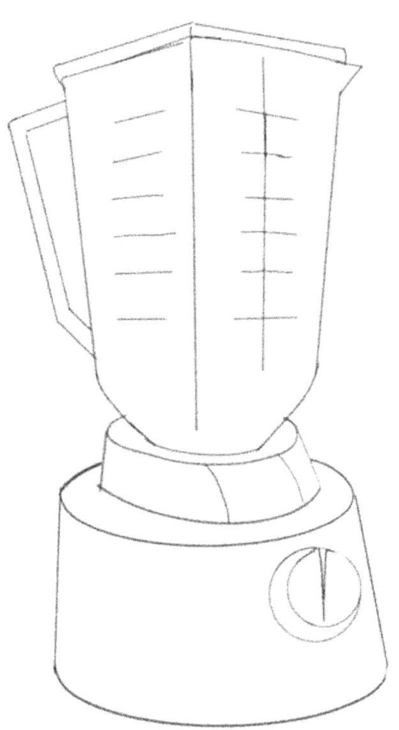

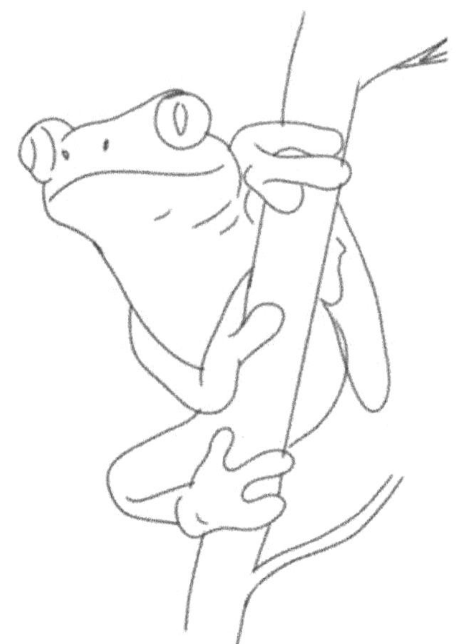

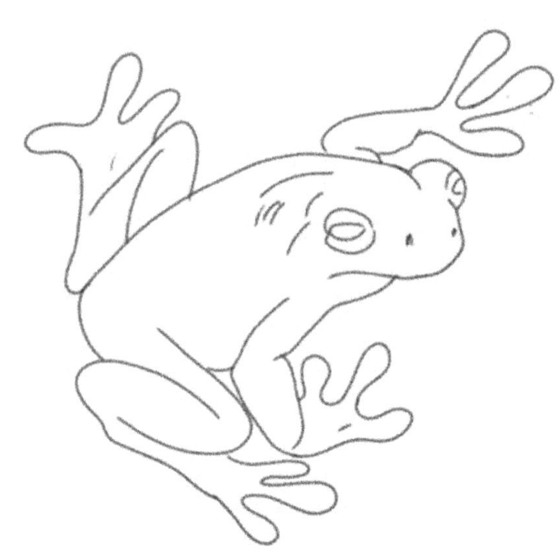

TREE FROG

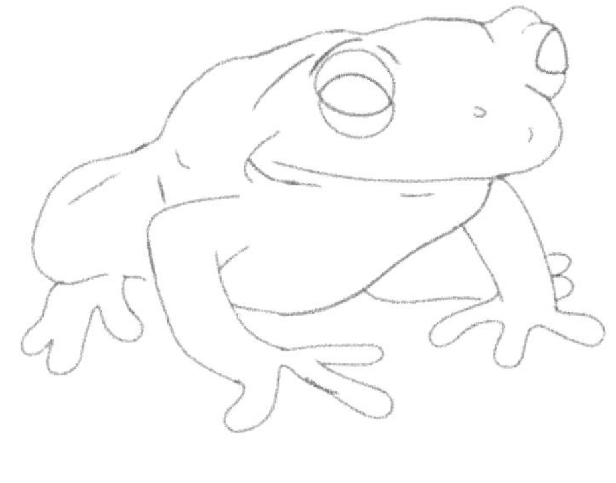

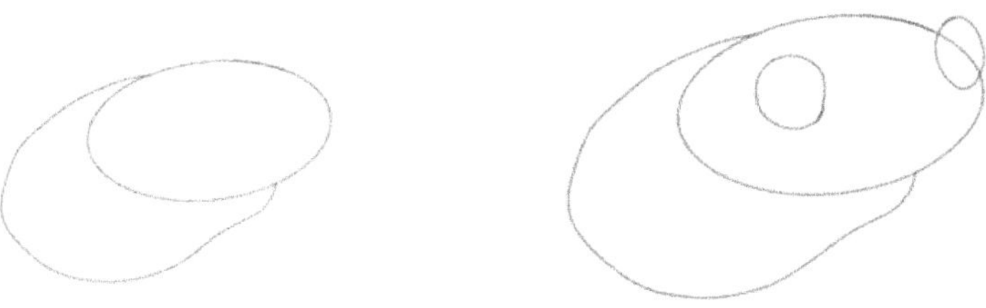

Draw the head and body of the tree frog using an oval and a curved line.

Draw two ovals of different sizes for the eyes on top of the frog's head.

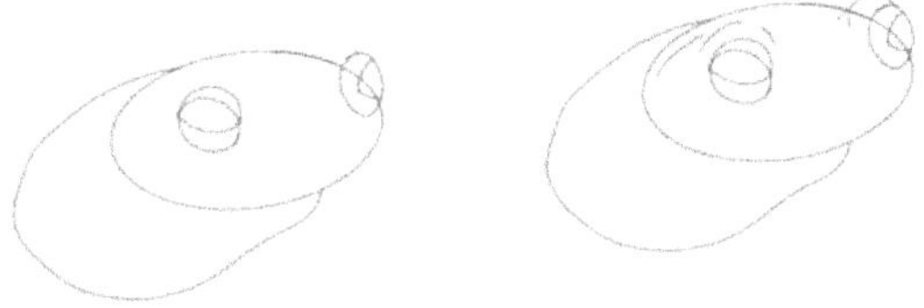

Draw smaller ovals inside the ovals you drew, and add bent lines near the eyes.

Draw dots for the nose and a curvy line for the mouth. To show wrinkles, add more lines near the eyes.

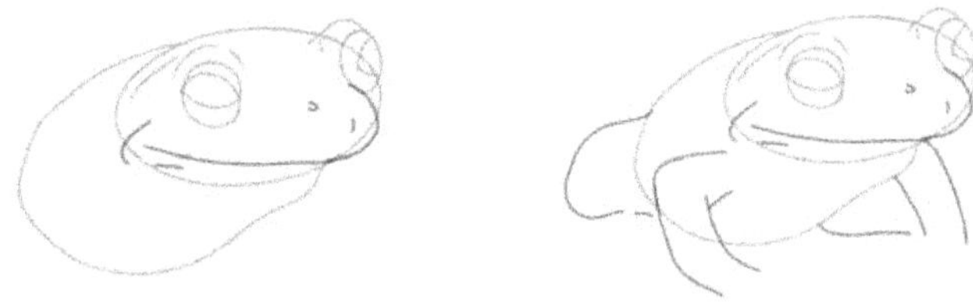

You should draw lines that are straight and curved To sketch the front and back legs of the frog.

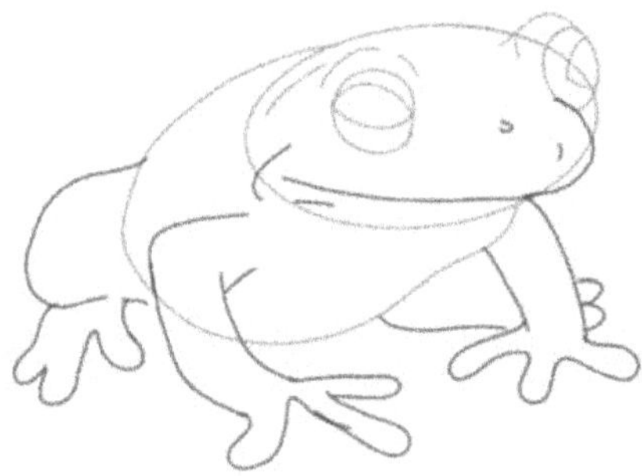

Use curved lines to draw the fingers on the frog's front paws. Use rounded lines to draw the toes on the frog's back leg.

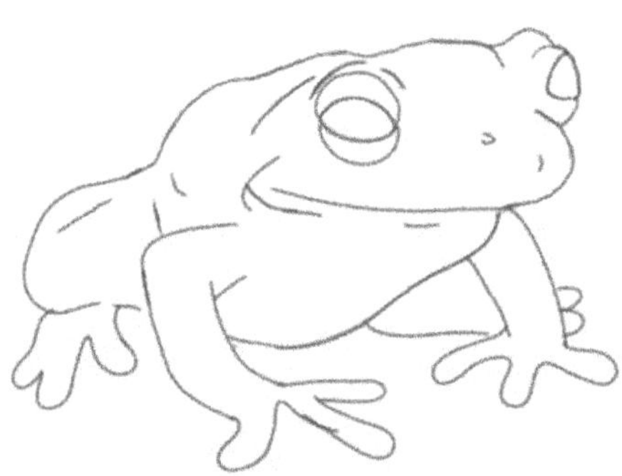

Use the eraser to get rid of the extra lines and to redo rough details

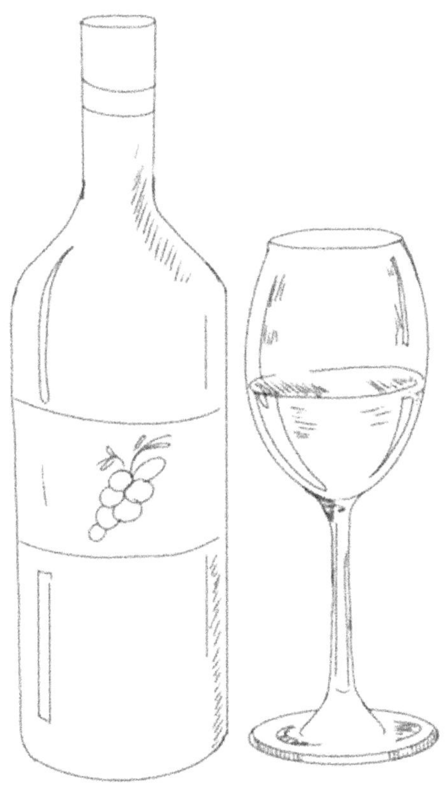

WINE BOTTLE AND GLASSES

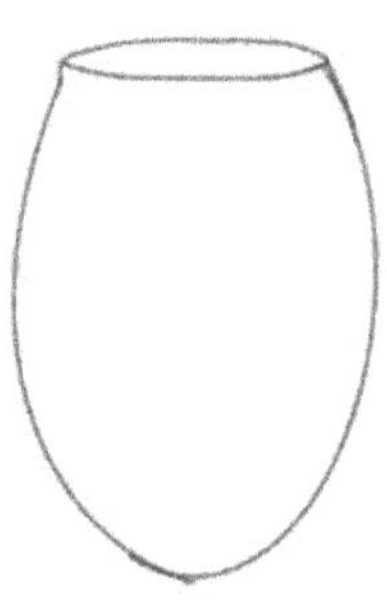

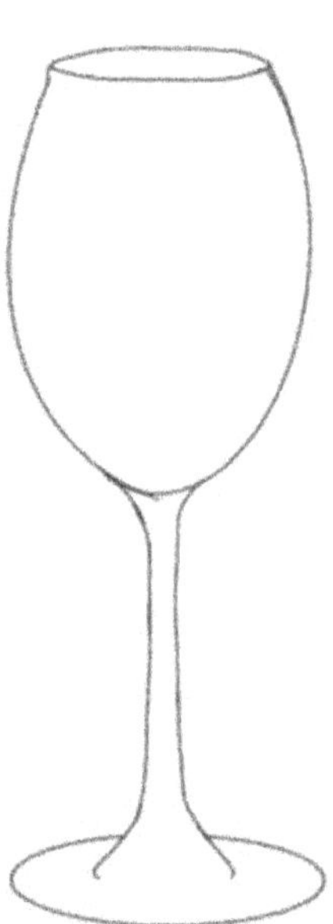

Make a simple circle for the glass's bowl, and then connect lines for the base.

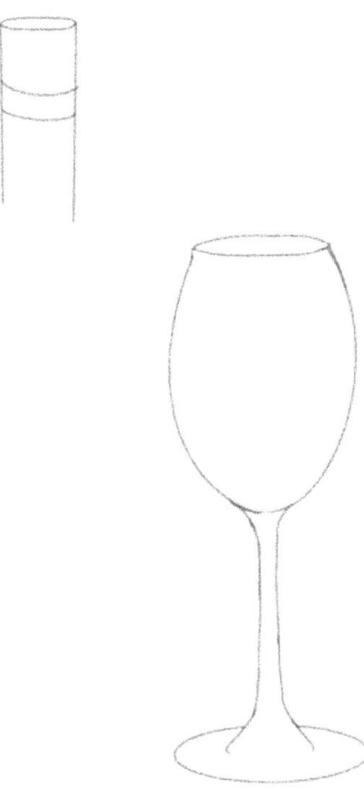

Then, draw a thin, straight line for the stem and an oval for the foot at the bottom. Next, we draw the tall stem of the wine bottle. Then add the wine bottle's big part.

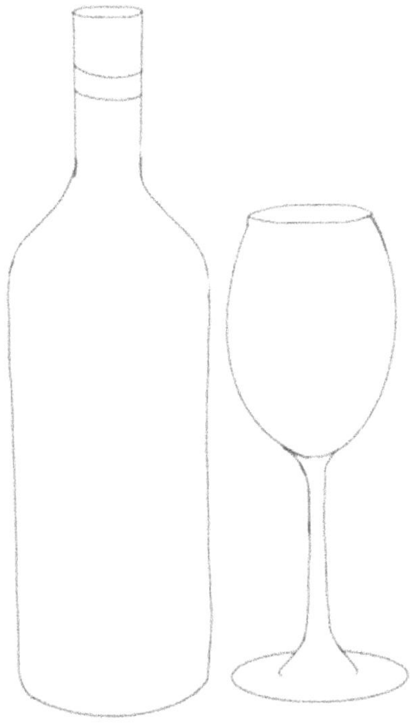

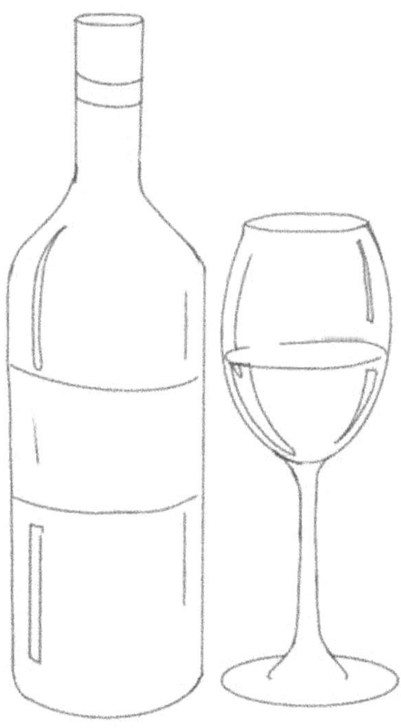

Let's pour half a glass of red wine into the glass. And draw some lines on the glass and bottle to make them look shiny and detailed.

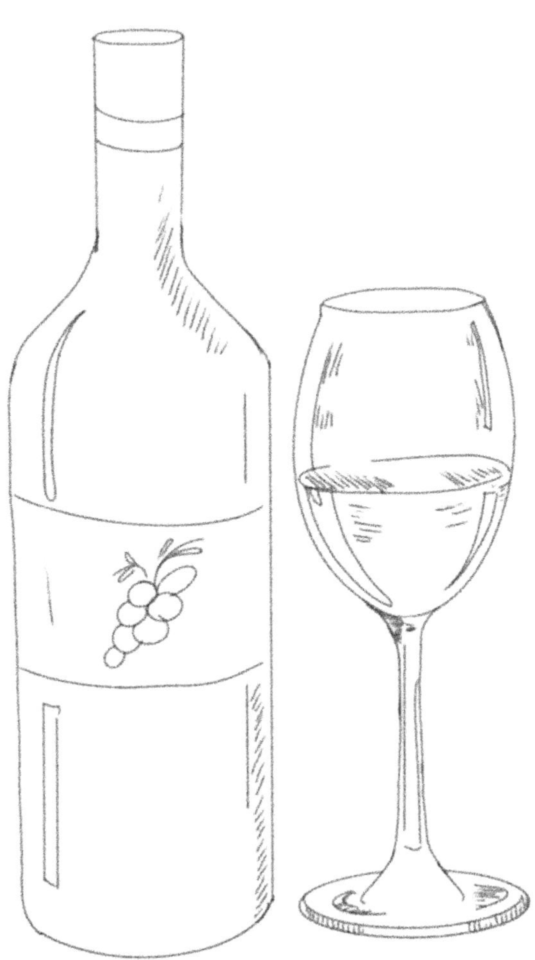

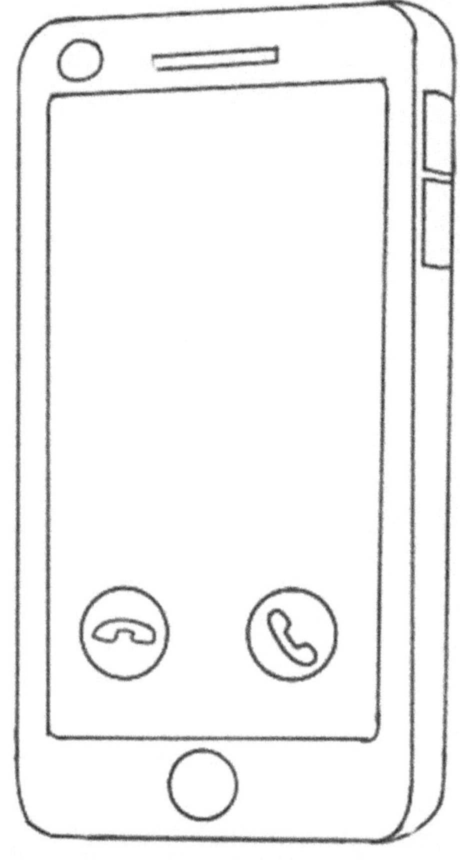

CELL PHONE

Use four straight lines to draw a rectangle the shape of a phone, be careful to make the sides round and not sharply curved. if they are, erase the edges and begin to round them up.

Fill in another straight line at the right side of the phone that connects to connect it to the round corner at the bottom of the phone.

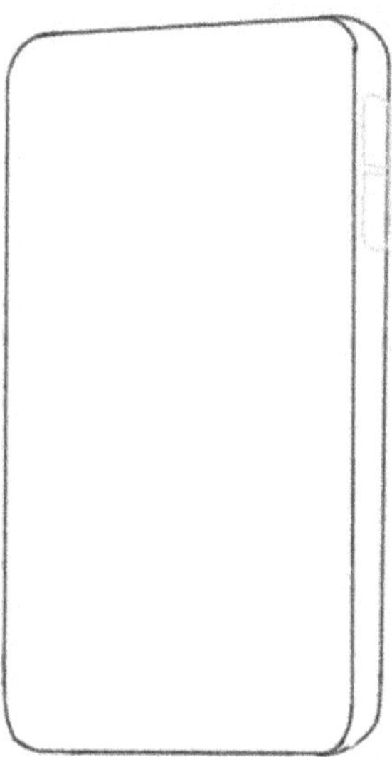

Put in two small rectangles on the side of the phone to show where the volume and power button are

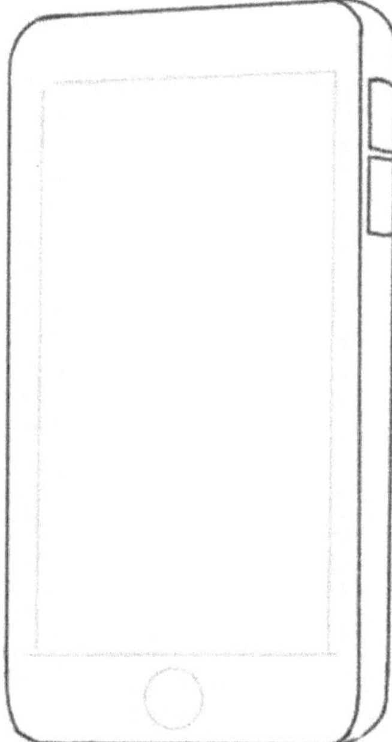

Draw a rectangle on the front of the phone with rounded sides to outline the screen. To make the "Home" button, draw a small square with rounded corners under it.

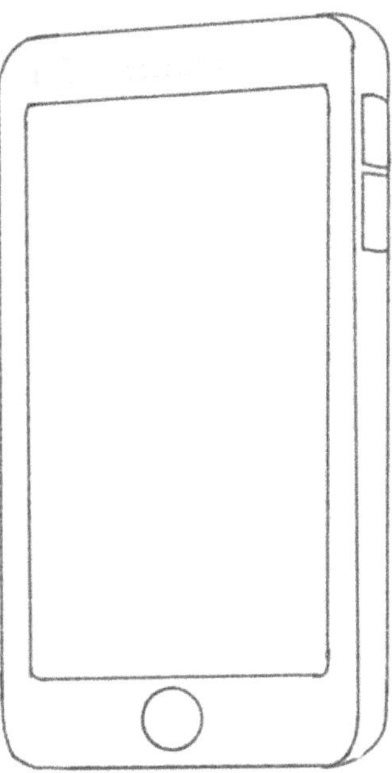

At the top of the phone, draw a small circle and a narrow rectangle with rounded sides to show where the camera and speakers are

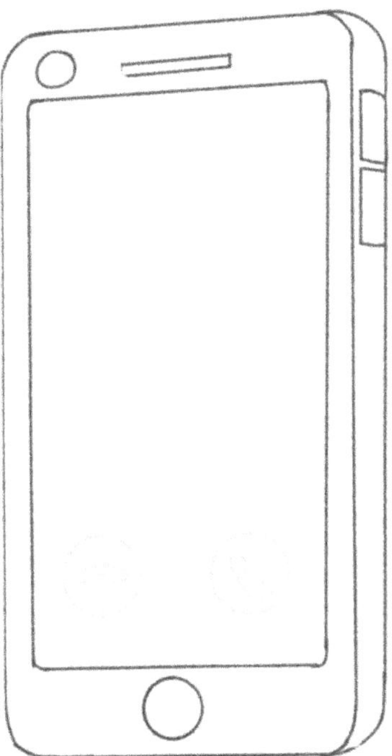

Draw two small circles in the bottompart of the screen for call options to answer the call.

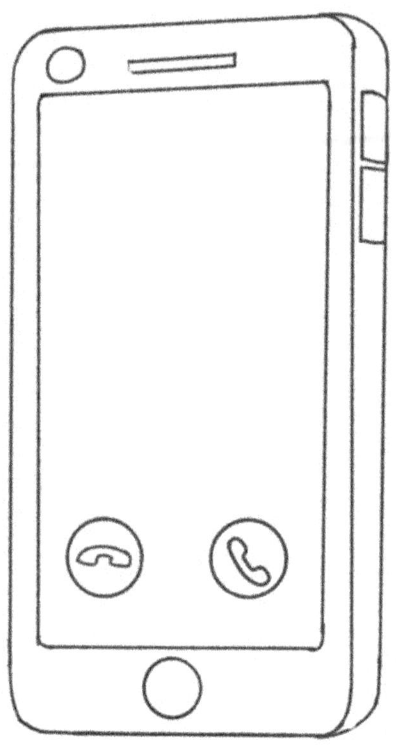

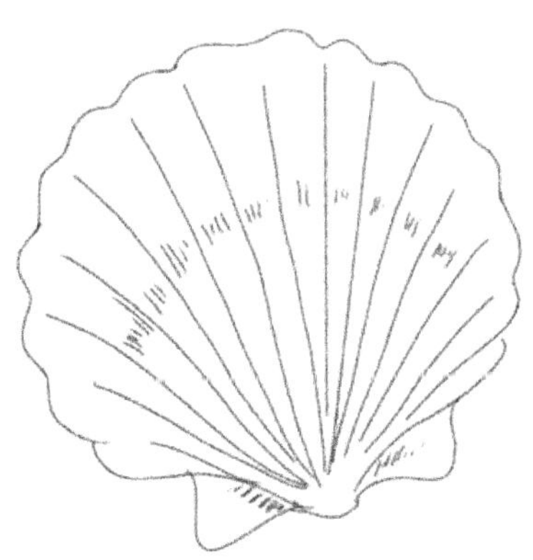
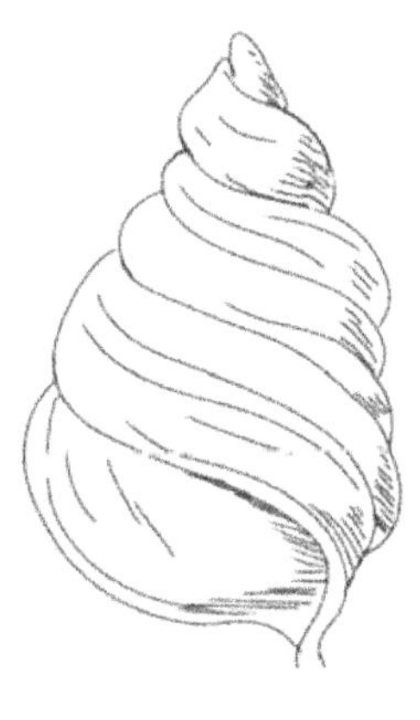
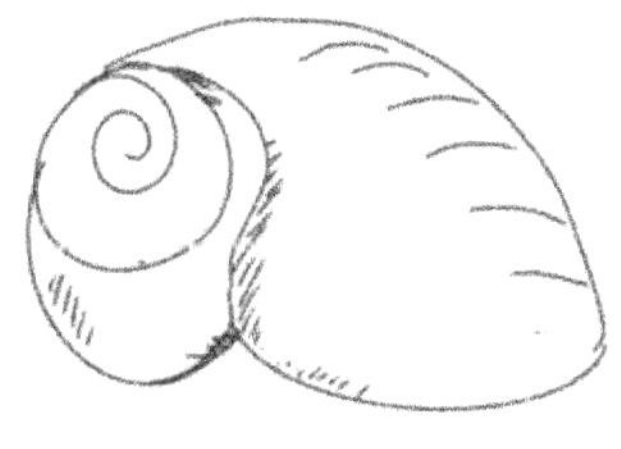

SEASHELLS

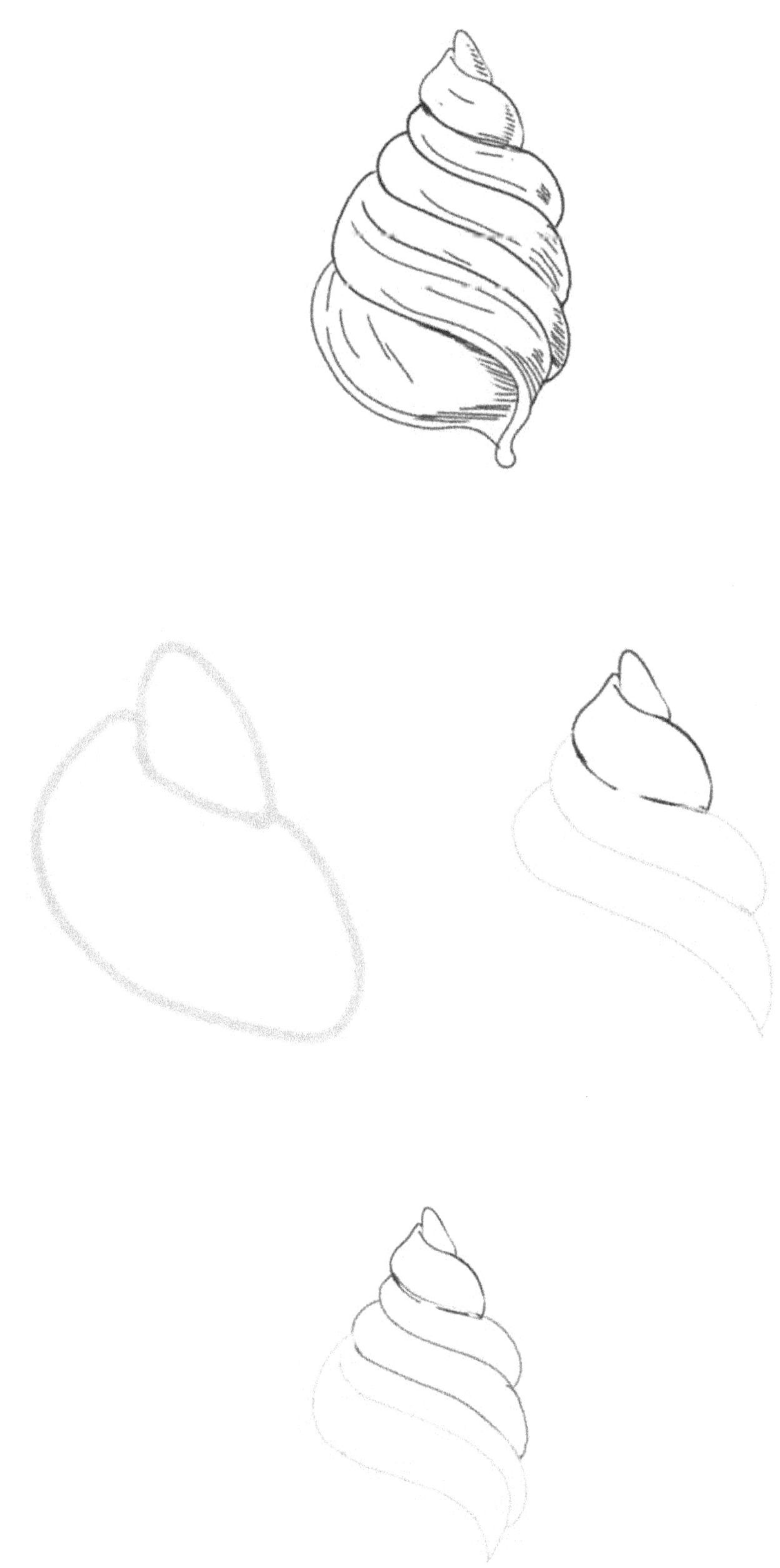

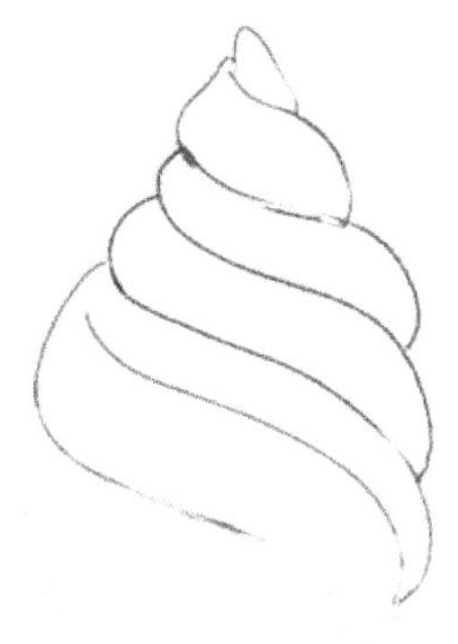

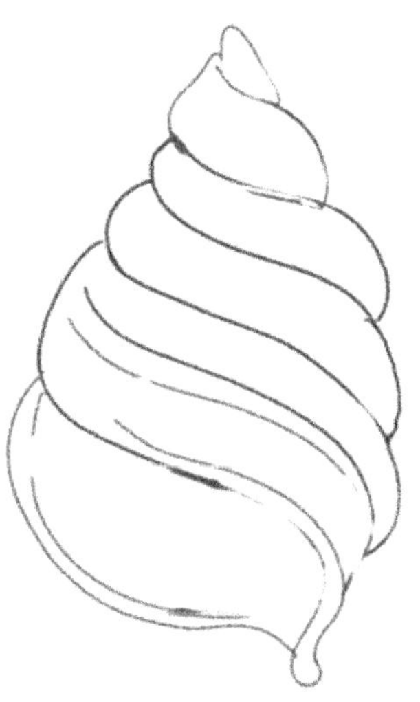

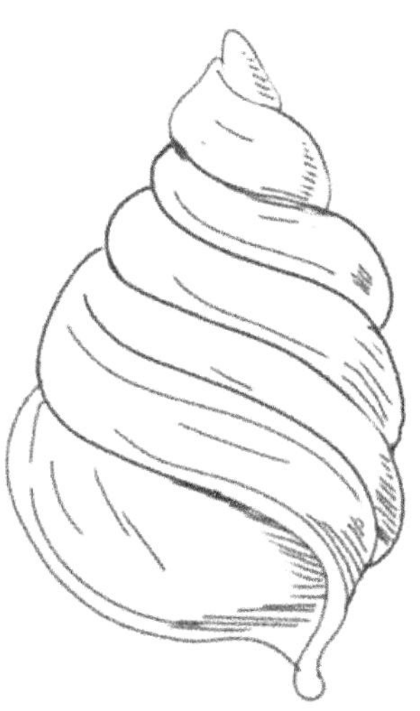

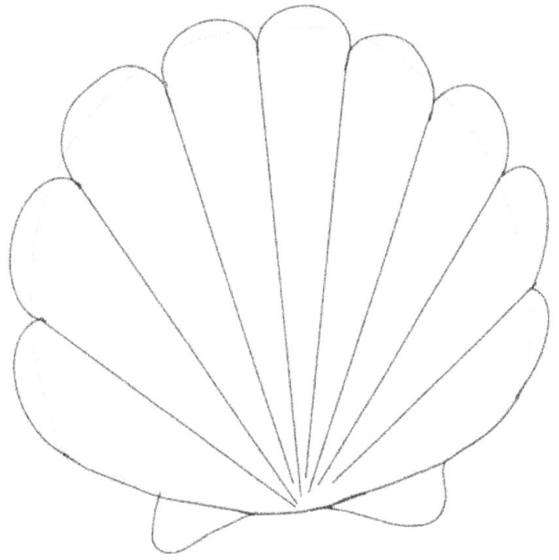

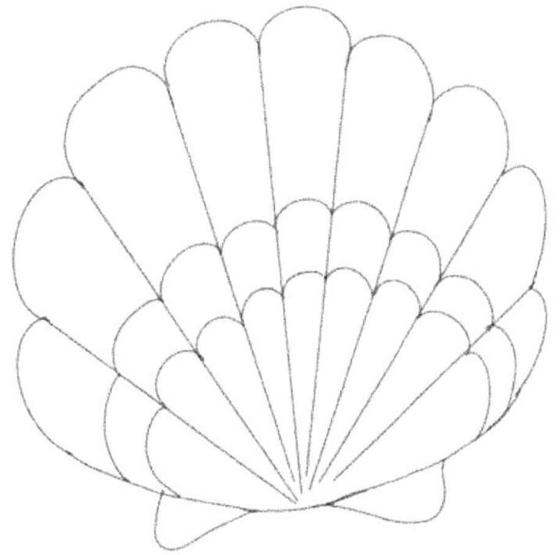

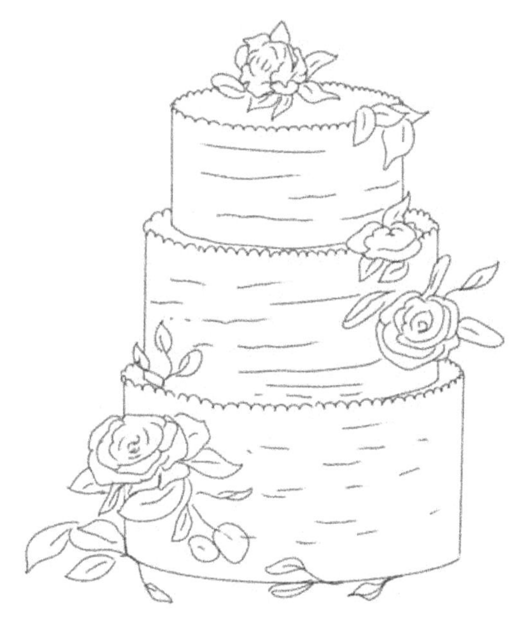

WEDDING CAKES

Start by making a large circle for the cake's bottom layer and then, draw two lines that go down from the circle you just made.

Once you've drawn those, you can draw two more ovals next to each other at the bottom of the lines until it looks like the picture you're copying. The top of the cake will be made of these ovals

Draw the top of your second level next.

Repeat the process with a smaller oval over your initial layer, build the same layer of cake and repeat until you have a three layered cake

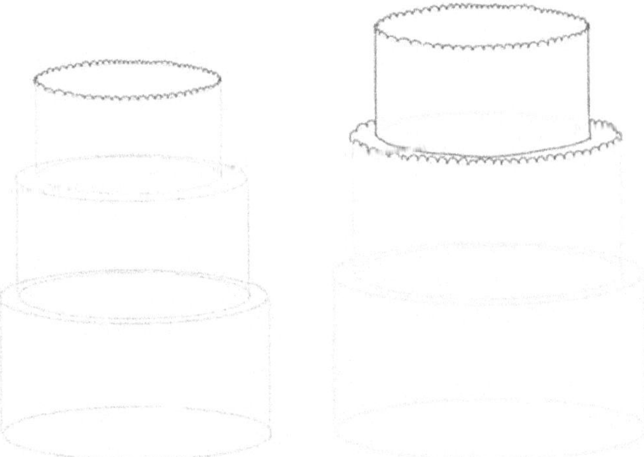

Next, add some detailing by erasing the oval lines and drawing some crummy lines to represent the icing, do these for all the layers of the cake.

Next, begin to add more details like flowers on the cake, if you find it hard to draw the flowers, you can choose something simple such as candles.

Finally, erase more details you wouldn't like to see.

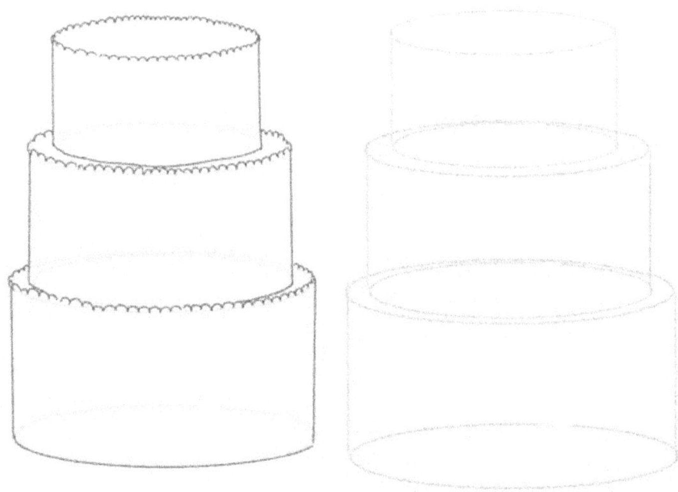

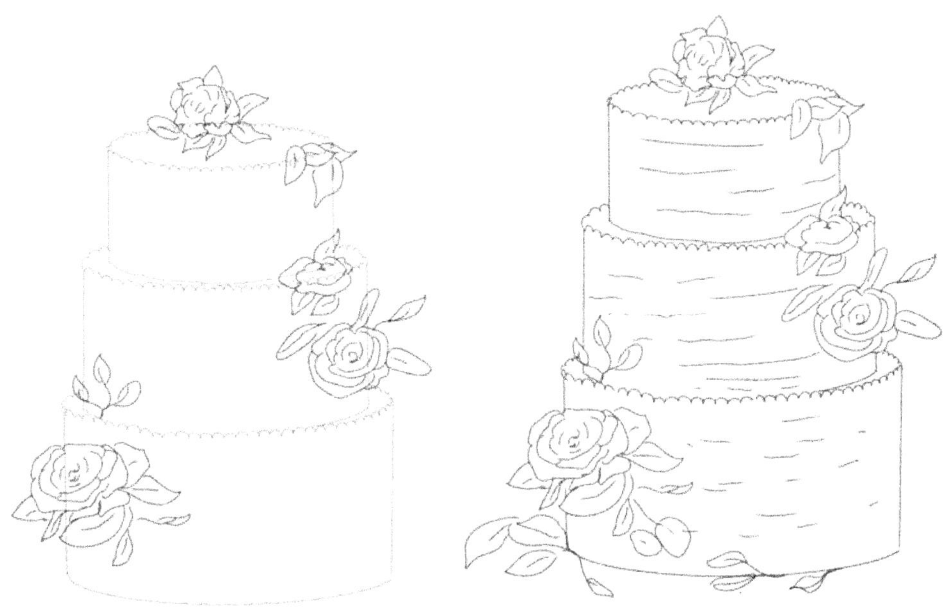

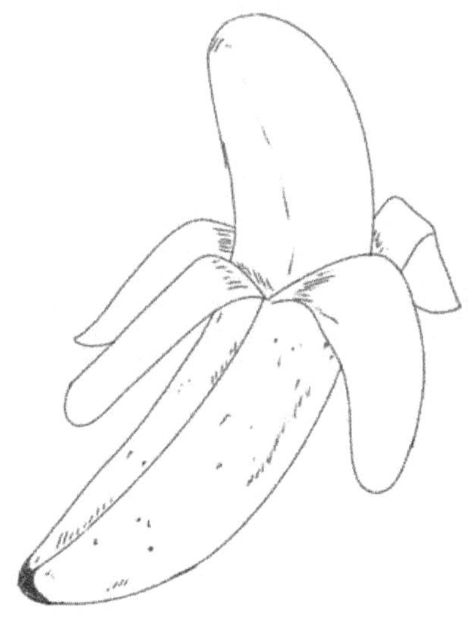

BANANAS

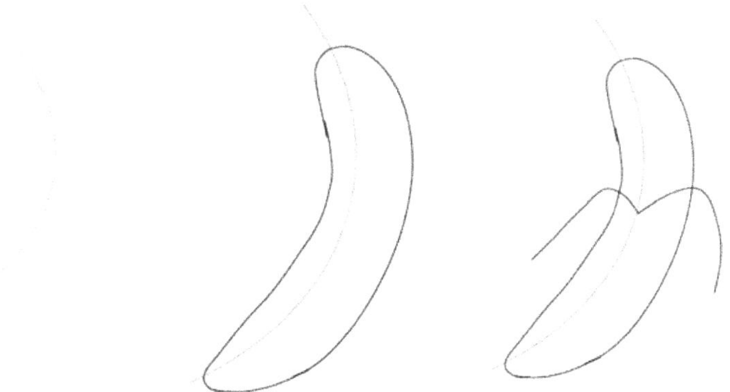

Draw a slightly slanted curved line and then draw the similar two curved lines on the right and left sides of this line.

Make sure the top and bottom ends of both the curved lines are connected, making a deep curve at the ends of the banana

Let's start drawing the banana peels. Start with a wide V with inwardly curved sides.

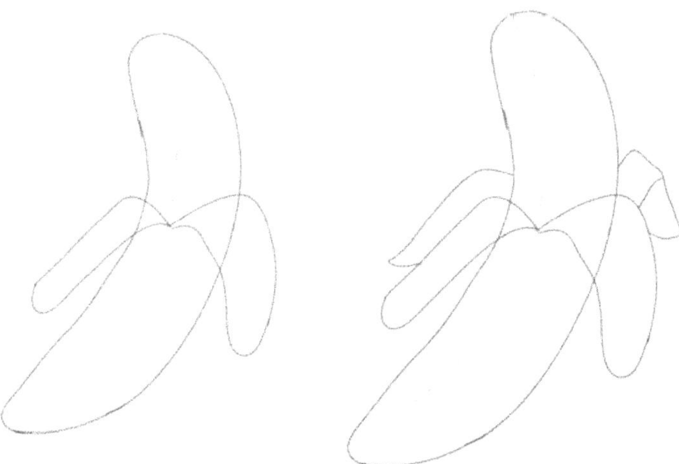

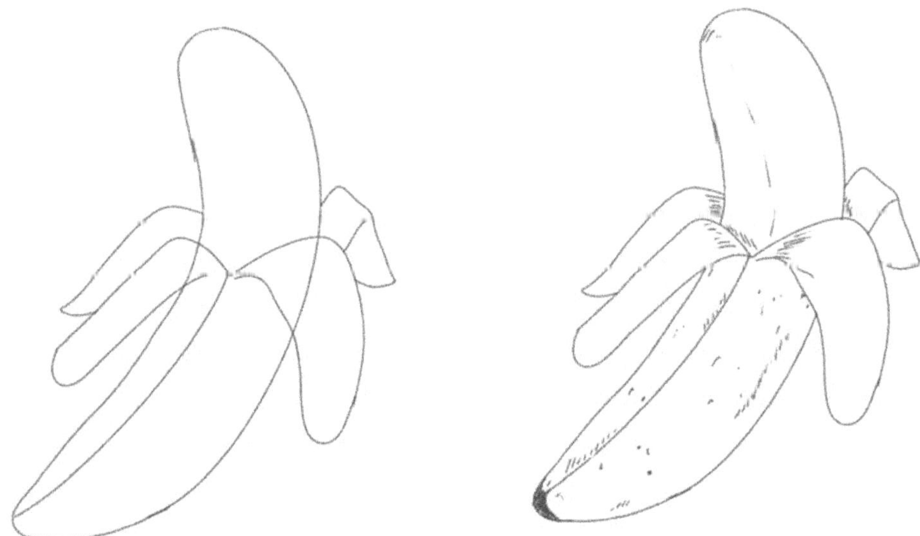

Starting from the ends of the V shape from the last step, draw one arc or a curved line going downwards on each side.

Start Drawing the Rear Peels of Banana: Draw a small and large curve or wave on the right and left sides of the banana, slightly above the front peels.

Draw the Centerline of the Banana Peel

Draw a centerline on the banana skin running down to the bottom part, exactly in the middle.

Add more details like dots to represent circles, then also some value for the dark spots

Concluded.

Epilogue

Congratulations! You've made it to the end of this drawing book guide, which makes me so happy. You set out on a creative trip with just a pencil and paper, and now you're a great artist who can do anything.

I hope this journey has been as beneficial for you as it has been for me. Please send me an email at and tell me what you thought of this book and what you did with it. Please send me photos of some of your best drawings through email. I can't wait to see what you come up with!

We aren't born with the ability to draw; we have to learn it. By practicing and being patient, anyone can learn to be a good artist. Keep getting better, continue to draw every day for twenty or thirty minutes. Start by trying to break things down into simple forms, figure out their force and rhythm, and write them down.

Keep thinking and making things,

Martha

About the Author

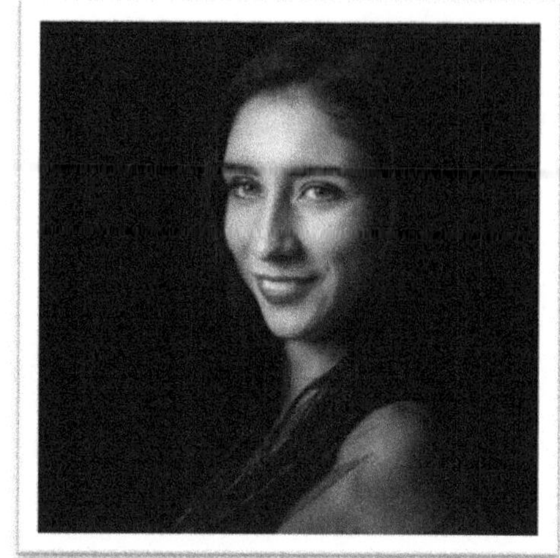

An acclaimed author and artist, Martha has always had a profound passion for creativity and the world of art. From an early age, her natural flair for design, painting, and all forms of artistic expression became evident.

Born and raised in a serene countryside, Martha's childhood was filled with wonder and inspiration. This is her third work, with each drawing explicitly drawn and each steps well explained.

Hope you enjoy it!

Get in touch

Feedback from our readers are always welcome.

General feedback: If you have any queries regarding this book, please email us at cactusbookspublishing@gmail.com and include the title of the book in the subject line.

Errata: If you discover an error in this book, we would appreciate it if you could notify us in the above address

Piracy: We would appreciate it if you could also inform us if you come across any unlawful copies of our works in any manner on the internet.

Becoming an Author: Please send us an email with a link to the material at cactusbookspublishing@gmail.com. If you want to be an author and there is a topic in which you have experience and would want to write or contribute to a book.

About the Author

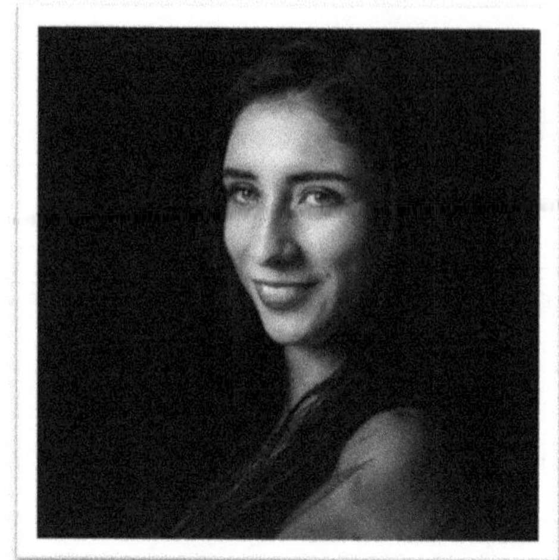

An acclaimed author and artist, Maggie has always had a profound passion for creativity and the world of art. From an early age, her natural flair for design, painting, and all forms of artistic expression became evident.

Born and raised in a serene countryside, Margret's childhood was filled with wonder and inspiration. This is her debut work, with each drawing explicitly drawn and each steps well explained.

Hope you enjoy it!

www.ingramcontent.com/pod-product-compliance
Ingram Content Group UK Ltd.
Pitfield, Milton Keynes, MK11 3LW, UK
UKHW061706190726
13853UKWH00008B/2440

9 789787 816592